HUMAN RIGHTS: BACKGROUND AND ISSUES

BIRTHRIGHT CITIZENSHIP IN THE UNITED STATES

ANALYSES AND PERSPECTIVES

HUMAN RIGHTS: BACKGROUND AND ISSUES

Additional books in this series can be found on Nova's website under the Series tab.

Additional e-books in this series can be found on Nova's website under the eBooks tab.

HUMAN RIGHTS: BACKGROUND AND ISSUES

BIRTHRIGHT CITIZENSHIP IN THE UNITED STATES

ANALYSES AND PERSPECTIVES

GARRETT MANNING
EDITOR

NOVINKA
New York

NOTICE TO THE READER

Library of Congress Cataloging-in-Publication Data

ISBN: 978-1-63485-258-6

Published by Nova Science Publishers, Inc. † New York

CONTENTS

Preface		**vii**
Chapter 1	Birthright Citizenship and Children Born in the United States to Alien Parents: An Overview of the Legal Debate *Alexandra M. Wyatt*	**1**
Chapter 2	Birthright Citizenship under the 14th Amendment of Persons Born in the United States to Alien Parents *Margaret Mikyung Lee*	**33**
Chapter 3	Testimony of Lino A. Graglia, A.W. Walker Centennial Chair in Law, University of Texas at Austin School of Law. Hearing on "Birthright Citizenship: Is It the Right Policy for America?"	**63**
Chapter 4	Testimony of Dr. John C. Eastman, Founding Director, the Claremont Institute Center for Constitutional Jurisprudence. Hearing on "Birthright Citizenship: Is It the Right Policy for America?"	**67**
Chapter 5	Statement of Jon Feere, Legal Policy Analyst, Center for Immigration Studies. Hearing on "Birthright Citizenship: Is It the Right Policy for America?"	**83**

Chapter 6	Testimony of Richard Cohen, President, Southern Poverty Law Center. Hearing on "Birthright Citizenship: Is It the Right Policy for America?"	**107**
Index		**113**

PREFACE

The first clause of the Fourteenth Amendment to the U.S. Constitution, known as the Citizenship Clause, provides that "[a]ll persons born or naturalized in the United States, and subject to the jurisdiction thereof, are citizens of the United States and of the State wherein they reside." This generally has been taken to mean that any person born in the United States automatically gains U.S. citizenship, regardless of the citizenship or immigration status of the person's parents, with limited exceptions such as children born to recognized foreign diplomats. The current rule is often called "birthright citizenship." However, driven in part by concerns about unauthorized immigration, some have questioned this understanding of the Citizenship Clause, and in particular the meaning of "subject to the jurisdiction [of the United States]." This book traces the history of birthright citizenship under U.S. law and discusses some of the legislation in recent Congresses intended to alter it.

In: Birthright Citizenship …
Editor: Garrett Manning

ISBN: 978-1-63485-258-6

Chapter 1

BIRTHRIGHT CITIZENSHIP AND CHILDREN BORN IN THE UNITED STATES TO ALIEN PARENTS: AN OVERVIEW OF THE LEGAL DEBATE*

Alexandra M. Wyatt

SUMMARY

The first clause of the Fourteenth Amendment to the U.S. Constitution, known as the Citizenship Clause, provides that "[a]ll persons born or naturalized in the United States, and subject to the jurisdiction thereof, are citizens of the United States and of the State wherein they reside." This generally has been taken to mean that any person born in the United States automatically gains U.S. citizenship, regardless of the citizenship or immigration status of the person's parents, with limited exceptions such as children born to recognized foreign diplomats. The current rule is often called "birthright citizenship."

However, driven in part by concerns about unauthorized immigration, some have questioned this understanding of the Citizenship Clause, and in particular the meaning of "subject to the jurisdiction [of the United States]." Proponents of a narrower reinterpretation of that phrase argue that the term "jurisdiction" can have multiple meanings, and that in the Citizenship Clause, "jurisdiction" should be read to mean

* This is an edited, reformatted and augmented version of a Congressional Research Service, Publication No. R44251, dated October 28, 2015.

"complete jurisdiction" based on undivided allegiance and the mutual consent of the sovereign and the subject. This has been termed a "consensual" approach to citizenship. Conversely, proponents of the conventional view interpret the term "jurisdiction" to mean territorial jurisdiction, that is, the authority of a sovereign to enforce its laws within its boundaries. Under the conventional rule, citizenship is ascribed to a person at birth on the basis of the geographic location of that person's birth in the United States. This birthright citizenship rule has sometimes been termed an "ascriptive" approach to citizenship.

Proponents of either side of this legal debate argue that a variety of sources and arguments support their respective positions. The two approaches differ in their interpretations of pre-Revolutionary English common law, pre-Civil War understandings of citizenship, the legislative history of the Civil Rights Act of 1866 and the Citizenship Clause of the Fourteenth Amendment, and subsequent case law. Two key Supreme Court cases in particular, *Elk v. Wilkins* (1884) and *United States v. Wong Kim Ark* (1898), interpreted the Citizenship Clause. *Elk* held that a member of a recognized Indian tribe was outside the scope of the Citizenship Clause because he was born owing allegiance to the tribe, rather than the United States, and the tribe was a political community not fully subject to the jurisdiction of the United States. *Wong Kim Ark* held that a person born in the United States to resident aliens became a U.S. citizen at birth, even when the person's parents were barred from ever naturalizing. However, some argue that *Wong Kim Ark*'s statements limiting the exceptions to birthright citizenship were not necessary to its holding, and that no Supreme Court case has ever squarely held that the Citizenship Clause requires a broad view of jurisdiction that extends birthright citizenship to children of unlawfully or temporarily present aliens. Twentieth and 21st century case law also can be seen to support the conventional interpretation of the Citizenship Clause, but again, not in direct case holdings.

Bills have been introduced since the early1990s to deny birthright citizenship to persons born in the United States to aliens other than lawful permanent residents. While a few proposals have suggested constitutional amendments, most seek to change the birthright citizenship rule by statute. It would likely fall to federal courts to determine whether such a statute could be upheld as constitutional. The weight of the legislative history of the Fourteenth Amendment, the analysis and discussion in *Wong Kim Ark*, the statements in various cases defining "jurisdiction" more often on the basis of territory rather than undivided allegiance, and the embrace of the prevailing birthright citizenship interpretation by more than a century of subsequent law, would probably factor against the constitutionality of a statute limiting birthright citizenship. Nevertheless, the scope of the guarantee of the Citizenship Clause remains a legal question of great interest and importance to many.

INTRODUCTION

In recent years, some scholars, legislators, and others have proposed to reexamine and potentially reinterpret the U.S. Constitution's Citizenship Clause to change and limit the current rule of conferring U.S. citizenship at birth to any person born in the United States, or "birthright citizenship."[1] The Citizenship Clause is the first clause of the Fourteenth Amendment, and states: "All persons born or naturalized in the United States, and subject to the jurisdiction thereof, are citizens of the United States and of the State wherein they reside...."[2] The policy debates on the topic of birthright citizenship are far-ranging, driven by concerns regarding unauthorized immigration,[3] global antiterrorism efforts,[4] reports of "birth tourism,"[5] and congressional redistricting,[6] among other issues. The legal debates, however, center squarely on the six words in the middle of the Citizenship Clause: "and subject to the jurisdiction thereof."

The Citizenship Clause has conventionally been taken to require U.S. citizenship generally to be accorded automatically to any child born within the United States,[7] regardless of the citizenship or status of the child's parents. The "subject to the jurisdiction thereof" language has been interpreted to impose limited exceptions, such as for children of diplomats and foreign ministers (who are accorded immunity from U.S. law).[8] This interpretation flows from the English common law doctrine of *jus soli* ("right of soil"), under which a person's nationality at birth is determined by the territory within which the person was born. The alternative doctrine of *jus sanguinis* ("right of blood"), which determines a person's nationality by descent, is now the more common general system outside of North and South America.[9] However, each system's adherents have incorporated some elements of the other, with few purely adopting one or the other.[10]

The *jus soli* interpretation of the Citizenship Clause is recognized in a number of judicial decisions;[11] however, arguably, no case has ever directly held whether the Citizenship Clause extends to children of aliens who are present in the United States unlawfully. The factual scenarios of the key cases interpreting the Citizenship Clause, *Elk v. Wilkins* (1884)[12] and *United States v. Wong Kim Ark* (1898),[13] involved Native Americans and children of domiciled resident aliens, respectively. *Elk* found that members of Indian tribes were not granted U.S. citizenship by the Fourteenth Amendment (a situation which was eventually remedied by statute[14]), while *Wong Kim Ark* found that the child of Chinese citizens residing in San Francisco had become a U.S. citizen at the time of his birth and therefore was not subject to the Chinese Exclusion Acts of the time.

Some scholarship in the past few decades has argued that the phrase "and subject to the jurisdiction thereof" in the Citizenship Clause was in fact intended by the framers of the Fourteenth Amendment to include only those children born to lawfully present or lawfully resident aliens, and not children of unauthorized or nonimmigrant aliens.[15] These arguments have been embraced by some legislators, who have introduced bills since the early 1990s seeking to change the *jus soli* rule in various ways.[16] Many of these bills target Section 301 of the Immigration and Nationality Act (INA), which tracks the language of the Citizenship Clause and states: "The following shall be nationals and citizens of the United States at birth: (a) a person born in the United States, and subject to the jurisdiction thereof...."[17]

Any statute reinterpreting the Citizenship Clause to exclude children of certain aliens would face judicial review by federal courts. Because of the core constitutional principles involved, it seems probable that any case on such a statute could reach the Supreme Court. The Court could find such a statute constitutional if it interpreted the "subject to the jurisdiction" language of the Citizenship Clause to exclude the children of certain aliens from the scope of the Clause's protection. To uphold a statute limiting birthright citizenship, it would also appear that the Court would have to find either (1) that the discussion in *Wong Kim Ark* apparently supporting the conventional interpretation of birthright citizenship was mere dicta, not binding precedent, and the case's holding was limited to the facts of that case; or (2) that *Wong Kim Ark* incorrectly interpreted the Citizenship Clause, at least in some respects, and should be overruled. If a statute could not change the meaning of the Citizenship Clause, then a constitutional amendment, as some have proposed, would have the power to do so.[18] Proponents and opponents of the current birthright citizenship rule have marshalled a variety of arguments and historical records on all of these points.[19]

This report first sets the stage for analyzing the modern debates by providing a brief historical review of U.S. citizenship from the time of the founding through the Civil Rights Act of 1866 and the Citizenship Clause of the Fourteenth Amendment of 1868. It then describes the primary Supreme Court decisions analyzing the scope of the Citizenship Clause, as well as subsequent decisions generally reflecting the conventional understanding of birthright citizenship. This report then presents an overview of the main legal arguments for and against reassessing the scope of the Citizenship Clause, building on the history and judicial precedent described in previous sections.

In light of the various bills that have been proposed to modify birthright citizenship, this report closes by discussing the primary legal considerations that would determine whether any congressional action to restrict birthright citizenship of U.S.-born children of alien parents without constitutional amendment could be upheld.

HISTORICAL DEVELOPMENT OF U.S. CITIZENSHIP BY BIRTH IN THE UNITED STATES

U.S. Citizenship before the Civil War

The original framers of the U.S. Constitution referenced, but did not define, national citizenship. The Constitution required that a person have been a citizen of the United States for seven years to be a Representative and for nine years to be a Senator,[20] and that a person be a natural-born citizen or a citizen at the time of the adoption of the Constitution in order to be eligible to be President.[21] It also gave Congress the power to establish a uniform rule of naturalization, but naturalization refers to the manner in which a non-citizen acquires citizenship, rather than citizenship by birth.[22] Nor did the Naturalization Act of 1790 or subsequent acts until the Civil Rights Act of 1866 define citizenship by birth within the United States.[23]

In the absence of any statement in the Constitution or federal statutes that U.S. citizenship was acquired by right of birth in the United States, citizenship at birth generally was construed in the context of the English common law. [24] As noted by the Supreme Court, "[t]he interpretation of the Constitution of the United States is necessarily influenced by the fact that its provisions are framed in the language of the English common law, and are to be read in the light of its history."[25]

For example, in an 1824 inheritance case, the Supreme Court proceeded on the assumption that three girls born in the United States were citizens, although their father was an Irish citizen who never naturalized.[26] In 1830, the Supreme Court held that the law of England as to citizenship at birth was the law of the English colonies, and that a person born in New York after the Declaration of Independence on July 4, 1776 was a citizen of the United States, unless he was born in British-occupied territory, left for England as a minor, and did not elect to affirm his U.S. citizenship within a reasonable time after attaining his majority.[27] In another early case more directly on point,

Lynch v. Clarke, a New York court held in 1844 that Julia Lynch, born to Irish aliens while they were temporarily sojourning in New York, was a U.S. citizen.[28] In determining the appropriate national law to apply, the *Lynch* court looked to the traditional English common law doctrine of *jus soli*,[29] holding that by the "law of the United States, every person born within the dominions and allegiance of the United States, whatever were the situation of his parents, is a natural born citizen."[30]

These birthright citizenship principles were not extended to slaves, or generally to Native Americans.[31] Moreover, in the infamous 1857 case of *Dred Scott v. Sandford*, Supreme Court Chief Justice Roger B. Taney wrote that the Constitution "point[ed] directly and specifically to the negro race as a separate class of persons, and show[ed] clearly that they were not regarded as a portion of the people or citizens of the Government then formed,"[32] and held that the Constitution precluded both Congress and states from granting citizenship to descendants of slaves or people of African descent generally.[33] As such, the *Dred Scott* decision applied a rigid racial limitation on the *jus soli* doctrine.

The Civil Rights Act of 1866

Following the Civil War, Congress passed the Civil Rights Act of 1866.[34] The first section of that act repealed *Dred Scott*. It provided "[t]hat all persons born in the United States and not subject to any foreign power, excluding Indians not taxed, are hereby declared to be citizens of the United States...."[35]

Prior to passage of the act, Congress debated its effects on citizenship, particularly the language "not subject to any foreign power, excluding Indians not taxed."[36] Senator Lyman Trumbull, a lead sponsor, introduced lan[37]uage similar to the above but omitting the exclusion for "Indians not taxed" on January 30, 1866. Senator Trumbull explained that "[o]ur dealings with the Indians are with them as foreigners, as separate nations,"[38] and in response to an inquiry from Senator Edgar Cowen whether the provision would "have the effect of naturalizing the children of Chinese and Gypsies born in this country," responded: "Undoubtedly."[39] Notably, Senator Trumbull and Senator Cowen agreed that "the children of German parents" were citizens under what was then the current law, and disagreed over the effects of race, rather than alien status of the parents.[40] However, in other statements on the citizenship provision, Senator Trumbull discussed the requirements of citizenship to be enshrined by the provision in terms of "owing allegiance" to the United States, or similar conditions seemingly additional to geographic presence.[41]

The Fourteenth Amendment to the U.S. Constitution

The Civil Rights Act of 1866 was passed over President Andrew Johnson's veto on April 9, 1866, and the Fourteenth Amendment was introduced soon thereafter, in May 1866.[42] As passed in the House and introduced in the Senate, the proposed Fourteenth Amendment lacked a citizenship provision. Senator Benjamin Wade proposed an amendment that would remove the word "citizen" from what would become the "privileges and immunities" clause and replace it with "person," saying that "the word 'citizen' ... is a term about which there has been a good deal of uncertainty in our Government."[43] In the discussion that ensued, Senator Wade explained his understanding that the only instance in which "a person may be born here and not be a citizen" was "in the case of children of foreign ministers...."[44]

The Citizenship Clause was initially introduced by Senator Jacob Howard to read: "All persons born in the United States, and subject to the jurisdiction thereof, are citizens of the United States and of the States wherein they reside."[45] Senator Howard stated:

> This amendment which I have offered is simply declaratory of what I regard as the law of the land already, that every person born within the limits of the United States, and subject to their jurisdiction, is by virtue of natural law and national law a citizen of the United States. This will not, of course, include persons born in the United States who are foreigners, aliens, who belong to the families of ambassadors or foreign ministers accredited to the Government of the United States, but will include every other class of persons.[46]

Once again, Senator Cowen objected and inquired, "Is the child of the Chinese immigrant in California a citizen? ... [I]s it proposed that the people of California are to remain quiescent while they are overrun by a flood of immigration...?"[47] Senator John Conness, of California, responded: "The proposition before us ... relates simply to the children begotten of Chinese parents in California, and it is proposed to declare that they shall be citizens.... I voted for the proposition to declare that the children of all parentage whatever, born in California, should be regarded and treated as citizens of the United States....”[48]

Further debate proceeded largely on the topic of Native American status.[49] In that context, Senator Trumbull stated: “What do we mean by ‘subject to the jurisdiction of the United States?’ Not owing allegiance to anybody else. That is what it means. Can you sue a Navajoe [sic] Indian in court? Are they in any sense subject to the complete jurisdiction of the United States? By no means. We make treaties with them, and therefore they are not subject to our jurisdiction.”[50]

Despite the Citizenship Clause’s expansion of birthright citizenship to “all persons born ... in the United States, and subject to the jurisdiction thereof” regardless of race, *naturalization* remained racially restricted even after the Fourteenth Amendment was ratified in 1868; the Naturalization Act of 1870 extended the naturalization process to “aliens of African nativity and to persons of African descent,” but other aliens who were not “free white persons” remained excluded.[51]

Litigation Involving the Citizenship Clause

Slaughter-House Cases and Elk v. Wilkins

The first Supreme Court decision to interpret the new Fourteenth Amendment, known as “*The Slaughter-House Cases*” decision, was not focused on the scope and interpretation of the Citizenship Clause.[52] Among other conclusions, this landmark 1873 decision rendered the Privileges and Immunities Clause a “practical nullity”[53] in holding that it referred only to federal rights as designated in the Constitution or as necessarily implied as belonging to citizens of the United States, and did not forbid the states from withholding the privileges and immunities pertaining to state citizenship.[54] In the course of its decision, the majority stated that “[t]he phrase, ‘subject to its jurisdiction,’ was intended to exclude from its operation children of ministers, consuls, and citizens or subjects of foreign States, born within the United States.”[55] However, this statement is generally regarded as dicta, that is, a remark not controlling as precedent on later courts because it was made in reference to an issue not actually before the court.[56]

Elk v. Wilkins, decided in 1884, did target the meaning of the Citizenship Clause, although not with respect to children of aliens. John Elk was born a member of a recognized Indian tribe, but had separated from his tribe and “taken up his residence among the white citizens” of Omaha, Nebraska, although the petition in the case did not allege that he had ever been naturalized or taxed.[57] A local registrar refused to register Elk as a qualified voter, on the grounds that Elk "was an Indian, and therefore not a citizen of the United States."[58] The Supreme Court upheld the dismissal of Elk's case against the registrar, holding that the Citizenship Clause of the Fourteenth Amendment did not make members of Indian tribes U.S. citizens at birth, largely because of the tribes' special status as independent political communities.[59] It declared that a member of an Indian tribe was born owing allegiance to that tribe rather than to the United States, and tribes were not fully subject to the jurisdiction of the United States. The Court stated:

> The evident meaning of these last words ["subject to the jurisdiction thereof"] is, not merely subject in some respect or degree to the jurisdiction of the United States, but completely subject to their political jurisdiction, and owing them direct and immediate allegiance.
>
> ... Indians born within the territorial limits of the United States, members of, and owing immediate allegiance to, one of the Indian tribes (an alien, though dependent, power), although in a geographical sense born in the United States, are no more "born in the United States and subject to the jurisdiction thereof," within the meaning of the first section of the Fourteenth Amendment, than the children of subjects of any foreign government born within the domain of that government, or the children born within the United States, of ambassadors or other public ministers of foreign nations.[60]

United States v. Wong Kim Ark

To this day, the primary Supreme Court case on the meaning of the Citizenship Clause as to birthright citizenship remains *United States v. Wong Kim Ark*, decided in 1898.[61] Wong Kim Ark was born in 1873 in San Francisco and resided and worked in California.[62] His parents, who were Chinese citizens and ineligible to naturalize under then-existing law, returned to their home country in 1890.[63] When Wong Kim Ark returned to the United States from a several month visit to China in 1895, he was detained on his steamship when a customs agent (responsible for immigration enforcement at the time) declared that he was not a U.S. citizen and that he therefore was barred from entry by the Chinese Exclusion Acts.[64] The government argued before the Supreme Court that "subject to the jurisdiction" referred to those born within the political, not territorial, jurisdiction of the United States. It pointed to the *Slaughter-House Cases*, *Elk v. Wilkins*, international adoption of *jus sanguinis* rules, some historical documents, and policy grounds to argue for limits on citizenship.[65] Wong Kim Ark's attorneys raised a number of arguments in opposition, including common law jurisprudence, the purpose of the Fourteenth Amendment and its context following the Civil War, and principles of national sovereignty.[66]

More than a year after the case was argued, Justice Horace Gray found for Wong Kim Ark in an opinion that:

- traced the development of the English common law with regard to *jus soli*, and countered the argument that it had been superseded by *jus sanguinis*;[67]
- read the original Constitution's references to citizenship in light of the common law while reviewing pre-Fourteenth Amendment judicial decisions on citizenship;[68]
- delved into the legislative history of the Civil Rights Act of 1866 and the Fourteenth Amendment;[69]
- reviewed interpretations of the Citizenship Clause by lower federal and state courts[70] and the executive branch;[71]
- analyzed and distinguished the *Slaughter-House Cases* and *Elk v. Wilkins*;[72] and
- stated:

> The foregoing considerations and authorities irresistibly lead us to these conclusions: The Fourteenth Amendment affirms the ancient and fundamental rule of citizenship by birth within the territory, in the allegiance and under the protection of the country, including all children here born of resident aliens, with the exceptions or qualifications (as old as the rule itself) of children of foreign sovereigns or their ministers, or born on foreign public ships, or of enemies within and during a hostile occupation of part of our territory, and with the single additional exception of children of members of the Indian tribes owing direct allegiance to their several tribes. The Amendment, in clear words and in manifest intent, includes the children born, within the territory of the United States, of all other persons, of whatever race or color, domiciled within the United States.[73]

The Court declared that "[e]very citizen or subject of another country, while domiciled here, is within the allegiance and the protection, and consequently subject to the jurisdiction, of the United States," reading allegiance fairly broadly and indeed "independently of any domiciliation ... [or] renouncing any former allegiance...."[74] The enumerated exceptions to birthright citizenship, for children of foreign diplomats, foreign public ships, or hostile occupying enemies, and members of Indian tribes, were also reiterated on several occasions in the opinion.[75] Moreover, the birthright citizenship guaranteed by the Citizenship Clause could not be abridged by the Chinese Exclusion Acts or any other legislation: "The Fourteenth Amendment, while it leaves the power, where it was before, in Congress, to regulate naturalization, has conferred no authority upon Congress to restrict the effect of birth, declared by the Constitution to constitute a sufficient and complete right to citizenship."[76]

The Court's ultimate holding, on the specific facts of the case, was phrased more narrowly than the foregoing general pronouncements on *jus soli* generally:

> [A] child born in the United States, of parents of Chinese descent, who, at the time of his birth, are subjects of the Emperor of China, but have a permanent domicil and residence in the United States, and are there carrying on business, and are not employed in any diplomatic or official capacity under the Emperor of China, becomes at the time of his birth a citizen of the United States.[77]

Chief Justice Fuller and Justice Harlan dissented, objecting to the application of the English common law rule and urging a narrower view of allegiance and jurisdiction.[78] They emphasized a treaty and statute disqualifying Chinese parents and their children from naturalization.[79]

Twentieth and 21st Century Case Law on Birthright Citizenship

After *Elk v. Wilkins* and *United States v. Wong Kim Ark*, the meaning of the Citizenship Clause of the Fourteenth Amendment as to U.S. born children of alien parents was generally taken to be fairly settled. U.S. citizenship was and is automatically granted to any person born within the geographic United States, unless the person fell within a specific exception and therefore outside the "subject to the jurisdiction thereof" requirement of the Fourteenth

Amendment. The main exceptions are children born as members of recognized Indian tribes (now citizens by statute[80]), and children born to foreign diplomatic officers.[81] The alien status, or even unlawful presence, of a child's parent or parents has not been held to deny U.S. citizenship to a child born in this country.[82] Notably, in World War II, former California attorney general Ulysses S. Webb brought an unsuccessful test case seeking to overturn *Wong Kim Ark* and remove Japanese Americans from voter rolls on the theory that they were not citizens.[83] The U.S. Court of Appeals for the Ninth Circuit summarily affirmed the district court's dismissal of that case "[o]n the authority of the [F]ourteenth Amendment to the Constitution, § 1, making all persons born in the United States citizens thereof, as interpreted by the Supreme Court of the United States in *United States v. Wong Kim Ark* ... and a long line of decisions";[84] the Supreme Court did not grant review.[85]

Plyler v. Doe and "Jurisdiction"

The Supreme Court has not directly addressed whether the Citizenship Clause necessarily requires U.S. citizenship to be granted to persons born in the United States to unlawfully present aliens. However, it has made pronouncements arguably relevant to that question while addressing other issues. Perhaps most notably, in 1983, the Supreme Court decided *Plyler v. Doe*, holding that a Texas statute which withheld state funds for the education of children who were not "legally admitted" into the United States, and which authorized local school districts to deny enrollment to such children, violated the Equal Protection Clause of the Fourteenth Amendment.[86] Texas had argued "that the Equal Protection Clause directs a State to afford its protection to persons *within its jurisdiction*" and that "persons who have entered the United States illegally are not 'within the jurisdiction' of a State even if they are present within a State's boundaries and subject to its laws."[87] The Court disagreed, holding that "[t]o permit a State to employ the phrase 'within its jurisdiction' in order to identify subclasses of persons whom it would define as beyond its jurisdiction, thereby relieving itself of the obligation to assure that its laws are designed and applied equally to those persons, would undermine the principal purpose [of] the Equal Protection Clause ...."[88]

While the threshold inquiry in *Plyler* centered on the "person within [a state's] jurisdiction" language of the Equal Protection Clause, the Court also analogized that phrase to the use of "jurisdiction" in the Citizenship Clause, in a footnote, stating:

> Although we have not previously focused on the intended meaning of this phrase ["within its jurisdiction"], we have had occasion to examine the first sentence of the Fourteenth Amendment, which provides that "[all] persons born or naturalized in the United States, *and subject to the jurisdiction thereof*, are citizens of the United States...." (Emphasis added.) Justice Gray, writing for the Court in *United States v. Wong Kim Ark*, 169 U.S. 649 (1898), detailed at some length the history of the Citizenship Clause, and the predominantly geographic sense in which the term "jurisdiction" was used. He further noted that it was "impossible to construe the words 'subject to the jurisdiction thereof,' in the opening sentence [of the Fourteenth Amendment], as less comprehensive than the words 'within its jurisdiction,' in the concluding sentence of the same section...."
>
> Justice Gray concluded that "[every] citizen or subject of another country, while domiciled here, is within the allegiance and the protection, and consequently subject to the jurisdiction, of the United States." *Id.*, at 693. As one early commentator noted, given the historical emphasis on geographic territoriality, bounded only, if at all, by principles of sovereignty and allegiance, no plausible distinction with respect to Fourteenth Amendment "jurisdiction" can be drawn between resident aliens whose entry into the United States was lawful, and resident aliens whose entry was unlawful.[89]

In the same Equal Protection context, the Court in *Plyler* also recognized "[p]ersuasive arguments" for withholding benefits "from those whose very presence within the United States is the product of their own unlawful conduct," but was more skeptical of "classifications imposing disabilities on the minor children of such illegal entrants," who could not control their parents' conduct or their own status.[90]

Hamdi v. Rumsfeld and Presumption of Citizenship

In 2004, the Supreme Court was invited to reassess the automatic granting of U.S. citizenship to children born to aliens in the United States by several *amici curiae* briefs in *Hamdi v. Rumsfeld*.[91] That case presented legal questions about the rights owed to a U.S. citizen, born in Louisiana to Saudi parents, who had been detained in Afghanistan as an enemy combatant.[92] The briefs by the Eagle Forum Education & Legal Defense Fund[93] and the Claremont Institute Center for Constitutional Jurisprudence[94] argued that *Wong Kim Ark* had been read too broadly. The *amici* argued that the Citizenship Clause of the Fourteenth Amendment should instead be read to advance a legal concept of citizenship based on consent, of both the individual and the sovereign, embodied in the Clause's "subject to the jurisdiction thereof" language.[95] The Court declined the invitation and did not discuss the issue of granting American citizenship to children of aliens, although a dissent authored by Justice Antonin Scalia did refer to Hamdi as "a presumed American citizen."[96]

Cases on Birthright Citizenship in U.S. Territories

Several recent cases have touched on the meaning of "subject to the jurisdiction thereof" in assessing the scope of another phrase in the Citizenship Clause, "born ... in the United States."[97] For example, in *Tuaua v. United States*, decided in June 2015, the U.S. Court of Appeals for the D.C. Circuit held that "born ... in the United States" did not extend to those born in the U.S. territory of American Samoa.[98] In doing so, the court analyzed the geographic scope of the *jus soli* doctrine and applied both *Elk v. Wilkins* and *United States v. Wong Kim Ark*. The court viewed the English common law rule as defining the domain of the king broadly, with those born in, for example, the American colonies treated as subjects of the king; however, the court was "unconvinced ... that *Wong Kim Ark* reflects the constitutional codification of the common law rule as applied to outlying territories," since Wong Kim Ark was born in San Francisco and issues regarding geographical scope of the Citizenship Clause were not addressed.[99] Rather, the American Samoan plaintiffs were more analogous to Indian tribe members under *Elk v. Wilkins* in terms of being "significantly self-governing."[100] American Samoa's situation was, perhaps more importantly, determined to a significant extent by *The Insular Cases*, a series of decisions beginning in 1901 in which the Supreme Court addressed whether the Constitution, by its own force, applies in any territory that is not a state.[101]

Notably, the Circuit Court in *Tuaua* briefly addressed and dismissed an argument that Congress could change the interpretation of the Citizenship Clause by statute, without constitutional amendment, stating:

> The United States Government also argues, "even if Plaintiffs were correct that ... the Fourteenth Amendment should generally confer birthright citizenship [on persons born in American Samoa,] ... Congress's direct modification of that status by statute trumps that interpretation" ... (relying on Rogers v. Bellei, 401 U.S. 815, 828 (1971)). This argument is novel, if curious. Yet it erroneously conflates Congress's broad powers over naturalization with authority to statutorily abrogate the scope of birthright citizenship available under the

Constitution itself. Congress's authority for the latter is wanting. *See generally* Marbury v. Madison, 5 U.S. (1 Cranch) 137, 178 (1803) ("[T]he constitution is superior to any ordinary act of the legislature.").[102]

THE MODERN LEGAL DEBATE OVER BIRTHRIGHT CITIZENSHIP

The debate over American birthright citizenship for children of aliens has, of course, significant policy and political philosophy components—and real world consequences—which are generally outside the scope of this report. In focusing on the legal and constitutional aspects of the debate, the remainder of this report begins by briefly introducing the main competing perspectives and their respective approaches to analyzing the history, constitutional text, and case law developments summarized in previous sections. It then notes some legislative proposals to limit birthright citizenship and discusses how, if enacted, they would likely be assessed by the Supreme Court. Those who seek a reinterpretation of the Citizenship Clause would seem to face substantially greater legal and constitutional hurdles than those who would maintain the birthright citizenship status quo. Nevertheless, it is not necessarily clear that the question has been truly settled.

Two Competing Interpretations of the Citizenship Clause

There are, broadly speaking, two sides to the current legal debate over whether the Citizenship Clause of the Fourteenth Amendment requires the automatic granting of U.S. citizenship to all persons born in the United States, including those born to unlawfully or temporarily present aliens.[103] It would be futile to attempt a comprehensive review of the many statements cited and arguments made on both sides, but even a summary of selected points illustrates the deep philosophical differences underlying the legal disagreements. The following sections highlight a few of the principal themes, although a full examination of points and counter-points on the issues below—and others—is outside the scope of this report.

"Ascriptive" versus "Consensual" Conceptions of Citizenship

What is generally considered the majority view, embodied in applicable law and policy, is that the Fourteenth Amendment does require U.S. citizenship to be automatically conferred on "[a]ll persons born ... in the United States"; and that the phrase "subject to the jurisdiction thereof" excludes from that general rule only certain common-law-based exceptions to the *jus soli* doctrine, for those born in the United States to foreign diplomats, hostile occupying forces, or members of recognized Indian tribes. Legally, the "jurisdiction" referred to by the Citizenship Clause is territorial jurisdiction, which is the power of a sovereign to enforce its laws within its territorial limits.[104] This conventional interpretation has been called the "ascriptive" view (at least by some opponents) because it determines citizenship by the objective geographical circumstances of a person's birth.[105]

On the other side, some argue that the Fourteenth Amendment does not *require* U.S. citizenship to be automatically granted to persons born in the United States to aliens, especially those aliens who are present unlawfully or who are domiciled elsewhere.[106] The core of this argument is that the phrase "subject to the jurisdiction thereof" was intended to codify a limitation on the birthright citizenship principle that, in the words of two of its early proponents, "demanded a more or less complete, direct power by government over the individual, and a reciprocal relationship between them at the time of birth, in which the government consented to the individual's presence and status and offered him complete protection."[107] The "jurisdiction" referred to by the Citizenship Clause, in this view, is a more "complete" jurisdiction that entails undivided allegiance.[108] This opposing view has been called the "consensual" approach, as its proponents would "make political membership a product of mutual consent by the polity and the individual."[109] In short, as one of the aforementioned *Hamdi v. Rumsfeld* amicus brief argued unsuccessfully before the Supreme Court in 2004, "[i]t is not the physical location of birth that defines citizenship, but the express or implied consent to jurisdiction of the sovereign."[110] It is generally acknowledged that opposition to the conventional interpretation is the minority viewpoint.[111]

Divergent Interpretations of Common Law, Legislative History, Constitutional Text, and Case Law

Both sides of the birthright citizenship debate look back to colonial and pre-colonial times for evidence for their respective positions. Some legal writers favoring a narrower reinterpretation of birthright citizenship have emphasized statements in English common law cases referring to "aliens in amity"; they argue that even the common law doctrine of *jus soli* came to rely upon mutual consent between the citizen and the sovereign, and that the Fourteenth Amendment did not intend to abandon what they interpret as common law notions of consent.[112] Other consensualist legal writers say that to the extent the English common law made persons English subjects purely on the basis of the place of their birth, the American Revolution rejected this element of the English common law and enshrined more consensualist ideals of a social contract.[113] Consensualist legal writers have also emphasized the right of expatriation, or the voluntary ending of citizenship, as a corollary that they argue supports an allegiance based approach to gaining citizenship at birth.[114] Proponents of the conventional interpretation of the Citizenship Clause generally argue that the American Founders understood the English common law doctrine of *jus soli* to include only limited exceptions for children born to diplomats and hostile occupying forces, and that, as various passages in the *Wong Kim Ark* decision describe, this understanding of the *jus soli* doctrine informed the framing of the Fourteenth Amendment.[115]

Interpretations of the legislative history of the Citizenship Clause of the Fourteenth Amendment, and of its precursor language in the Civil Rights Act of 1866, are similarly divergent, even as to some of the very same passages in the *Congressional Globe*. As recognized by the Supreme Court, "the legislative history of the Fourteenth Amendment ... like most other legislative history, contains many statements from which conflicting inferences can be drawn...."[116] Those in favor of narrowing birthright citizenship often point to passages in the 1866 congressional debates referring to "complete jurisdiction"[117] or notions of "allegiance,"[118] arguing that the framers of the Fourteenth Amendment would not have understood today's unlawfully present aliens or their U.S. born children as meeting these requirements. However, the legislators' statements cited by consensualist writers were made largely, though not entirely, in the context of the exclusion from the Citizenship Clause of members of Indian tribes.[119] As proponents of retaining birthright citizenship point out, other indicia in the legislative history indicate that children of aliens were considered differently than children of Indian tribe members and were broadly intended to be included within the Citizenship Clause's scope.[120] The two sides also differ as to how the Civil Rights Act of 1866's language giving citizenship to all persons born in the United States "not subject to any foreign power" should be evaluated in interpreting the modified language in the Citizenship Clause of the Fourteenth Amendment.[121]

Within the consensualist camp, it appears that most argue that *Wong Kim Ark* could be interpreted narrowly, rather than overturned, in order to support reinterpreting the Citizenship Clause.[1] As noted above, Wong Kim Ark's parents had apparently established as firm a foothold in the United States as was legally available to them; the holding of the case referred to their "permanent domicil and residence in the United States" at the time of his birth, although the rest of the analysis and the discussion in the case ranged much more broadly. Proponents of the birthright citizenship status quo argue that the *Elk v. Wilkins* and *Wong Kim Ark* Supreme Court decisions in the 1800s essentially settled the meaning of the Citizenship Clause, in part by enumerating the few exceptions to the *jus soli* doctrine, which did not include the unlawful or temporary presence in the United States of a person's alien parents at the time of that person's birth.[123]

Supporters of the ascriptive and consensual viewpoints also debate, for example, whether other case law supports giving the term "jurisdiction" in the Citizenship Clause its more conventional and straightforward definition based on geographic territoriality, or a narrower and more context-specific definition based on allegiance and consent.[124] Supporters of the prevailing interpretation also argue that a broader interpretation of "jurisdiction" hews more closely to a textualist approach, and avoids having to draw an "elaborate construct" of consent and allegiance from contextual sources.[125]

Disagreement over Historical Precedent for Modern Immigration Issues

An argument often raised by those who wish to change the current rule of birthright citizenship is that illegal immigration, in the form it exists today, did not exist prior to the adoption of general immigration statutes, which was well after the adoption of the Fourteenth Amendment.[126] Some commentators have argued that "it is simply wrong to assert that there has ever been a conscious deliberate decision, by the framers of the Fourteenth Amendment or its judicial interpreters, to accord birthright citizenship under the [Citizenship] clause to children of illegal aliens."[127] Proponents of a narrower interpretation argue that the United States embraced a more open borders policy prior to the Twentieth Century,[128] and point out that the framers of the Fourteenth Amendment apparently did not discuss unlawfully present aliens per se, as recorded in the *Congressional Globe* (precursor to today's *Congressional Record*).[129] The *Wong Kim Ark* decision also did not expressly declare that the children of unlawfully present aliens were included within the scope of the Citizenship Clause, because Wong Kim Ark's parents had apparently been lawfully domiciled in San Francisco at the time of his birth.

On the other hand, the Chinese Exclusion Acts were a legal fact by the time the *Wong Kim Ark* case was decided,[130] and any Chinese citizen who entered the United States in violation of these Acts would have been unlawfully present. Violations of the Chinese Exclusion Acts were known by the time of *Wong Kim Ark* to have occurred, and some late nineteenth century writers believed they had occurred at a large scale.[131] Some modern commenters have also pointed to slaves imported in violation of the slave import ban that took effect in 1808,[132] or to socially isolated and generally unwelcome "Gypsies" allegedly entering the United States,[133] as nineteenth century precursors to today's unlawfully present aliens that would have been known to the framers and judicial interpreters of the Citizenship Clause. The discussion over whether modern illegal immigration is novel also raises broader issues regarding how to apply the Constitution to social conditions that may have been unanticipated by the framers.

Proposed Legislative Reinterpretations of the Citizenship Clause

Lawmakers in Congress, as well as state-level legislators and various interest groups, have offered proposals since at least the early 1990s to restrict automatic U.S. citizenship at birth.[134]

Some of these have taken the form of resolutions proposing to amend the Constitution,[135] but it appears that the more often proposed approach is to amend the Immigration and Nationality Act without constitutional amendment.

In 1995, a hearing was held on a collection of bills and resolutions to deny automatic citizenship at birth to children born in the United States to parents who are not citizens or permanent residents.[136] A decade later, another hearing was held involving the topic of birthright citizenship.[137]

More recently, companion measures entitled the "Birthright Citizenship Act of 2015" were introduced in both the House and the Senate. The bills would amend Section 301 of the Immigration and Nationality Act to provide, applicable prospectively as of the date of enactment, that:

> Acknowledging the right of birthright citizenship established by section 1 of the 14th amendment to the Constitution, a person born in the United States shall be considered 'subject to the jurisdiction' of the United States for purposes of subsection (a)(1) if the person is born in the United States of parents, one of whom is—

(1) a citizen or national of the United States;

(2) an alien lawfully admitted for permanent residence in the United States whose residence is in the United States; or

(3) an alien performing active service in the armed forces....[138]

In other words, if both parents were unlawfully present aliens or were present only on nonimmigrant visas or as refugees or asylees at the time of the birth of their child, that child would not be granted U.S. citizenship. At least one parent would have to be a citizen, a non-citizen national (such as an American Samoan[139]), a lawful permanent resident (i.e., green card holder), or actively serving in the U.S. armed forces in order for a U.S. born child to obtain citizenship at birth. An amendment with similar contents was offered in March 2015 to the Justice for Victims of Trafficking Act, but the amendment was not added to the bill.[140]

The House Judiciary Committee's Subcommittee on Immigration and Border Security held a hearing in April 2015 entitled "Birthright Citizenship: Is It the Right Policy for America?"[141] Attendees and witnesses at the hearing extensively discussed legal and constitutional issues of restricting birthright citizenship by statute, including much of the historical development, legislative history, and case law reviewed in this report.[142]

Legality of Narrowing the Citizenship Clause without Constitutional Amendment

It is generally acknowledged, even by those who would change it, that the current policy of automatically granting U.S. citizenship to essentially every person born in the United States is at least *permissible* under the Citizenship Clause.[143] This is because the Citizenship Clause sets a minimum guarantee, a floor above which Congress may but is not required to extend U.S. citizenship by birth to additional groups, as it has done for Native Americans and for children of U.S. citizens born abroad under certain circumstances. If, as many argue,[144] the current interpretation is *required* under the language and context of the Citizenship Clause and relevant judicial precedent, then a statute or other action purporting to reinterpret the Citizenship Clause more narrowly would be held unconstitutional, and a new amendment to the Constitution would be necessary to impose new restrictions on America's birthright citizenship policy.[145]

It would likely fall to the judicial branch to determine whether the Citizenship Clause would permit a narrower interpretation by Congress (or by the Executive Branch).[146] This determination could potentially require a court to weigh a number of complex considerations, including:

- canons of constitutional interpretation, including the degree to which textualist, originalist, traditionalist, prudential, and aspirational or ethical approaches should be applied to the Citizenship Clause;
- separation of powers, and each branch's relative authority to interpret—and particularly to limit—rights set forth in the Constitution, especially the Fourteenth Amendment;[147]
- stare decisis, or adherence to judicial precedent, and how to interpret and apply relevant cases; and
- the specific nature and language of the citizenship-limiting statute or other action under review.

Opinions on the most likely outcome of such a determination differ. Judge Richard Posner, of the U.S. Court of Appeals for the Seventh Circuit, stated in a 1996 concurrence that "[a] constitutional amendment may be required to change the rule whereby birth in this country automatically confers U.S. citizenship, but I doubt it. ... Congress would not be flouting the Constitution if it amended the Immigration and Nationality Act to put an end to the nonsense."[148] Some commentators have testified before Congress that they believe a statute denying birthright citizenship to children of unlawfully present aliens would likely survive constitutional challenge.[149] Others, however, have concluded that any of a number of legal and constitutional obstacles would more likely prove insurmountable to a narrower reinterpretation of the Citizenship Clause.[150]

Since automatic granting of American citizenship to all who are born here, without inquiring into parental origins or status, has been the practice and the law for more than a century, some supporters of the status quo have contended that a reinterpretation of the Citizenship Clause would mark a "seismic shift" in constitutional law.[151] The size of the policy change, in itself, could present an impediment to judicial support for the constitutionality of a citizenship-limiting statute. Opponents of reinterpretation could also urge a court to take into legal consideration what they view as practical, policy, or ethical considerations stemming from issues such as the potential for creation of a stateless subpopulation.[152] It has also been argued that "[t]he justices may also be reluctant to weaken a constitutional amendment explicitly designed to override a previous Supreme Court ruling—especially if that ruling was *Dred Scott*."[153] On the other hand, proponents of a narrower reinterpretation could potentially avail themselves of a number of practical and policy counterarguments; for example, some have asserted that a major divergence of modern circumstances from historical assumptions warrants a change from the prevailing interpretation.[154]

Congress's authority to reinterpret the Citizenship Clause, to exclude persons born in the United States to unlawfully or temporarily present aliens from its scope, would be significantly constrained if the *Wong Kim Ark* decision and subsequent case law were to be interpreted as having settled that issue in favor of those persons' inclusion. Factors that the U.S. Supreme Court generally considers when responding to a request to overrule precedent include whether that precedent "has proved 'unworkable' ..., the antiquity of the precedent, the reliance interests at stake, and of course whether the decision was well reasoned."[155] Ultimately, the Court "does not overturn its precedents lightly. Stare decisis ... is a foundation stone of the rule of law, ... [and] 'any departure' from the doctrine 'demands special justification.'"[156] However, if any discussion in *Wong Kim Ark* arguably extending beyond the citizenship of a person born to lawfully present and domiciled aliens is deemed mere dicta, unnecessary to the case's holding, then the Court would not be bound by it, although it could still weigh the dicta's persuasive value.[157]

Other precedent less specific to citizenship issues could pose legal obstacles to a reinterpretation as well. For example, courts would have to grapple with the meaning of "jurisdiction" as it has been interpreted in the context of the Equal Protection Clause, which follows the Citizenship Clause in the Fourteenth Amendment.[158]

Finally, any statute reinterpreting the Citizenship Clause would be far more difficult to uphold if it were designed to operate retroactively to remove or revoke any living person's U.S. citizenship. As stated by the Supreme Court in *Afroyim v. Rusk*, a 1967 case that held unconstitutional a statute that provided that a U.S. citizen would lose his citizenship upon voting in a political election in a foreign state:

> Citizenship is no light trifle to be jeopardized any moment Congress decides to do so under the name of one of its general or implied grants of power. ... The very nature of our free government makes it completely incongruous to have a rule of law under which a group of citizens temporarily in office can deprive another group of citizens of their citizenship. We hold that the Fourteenth Amendment was designed to,

> and does, protect every citizen of this Nation against a congressional forcible destruction of his citizenship, whatever his creed, color, or race. Our holding does no more than to give to this citizen that which is his own, a constitutional right to remain a citizen in a free country unless he voluntarily relinquishes that citizenship.[159]

However, Congress tends to propose applying birthright citizenship restrictions only prospectively, which, as a consequence, would not result in the loss of citizenship by any person already a citizen.[160] Nevertheless, a number of hurdles to such bills likely remain, including but not limited to the weight of the legislative history of the Fourteenth Amendment, the extensive discussion in *Wong Kim Ark*, the statements in various cases defining "jurisdiction" more often on the basis of territory rather than undivided allegiance, and the embrace of the prevailing birthright citizenship interpretation by more than a century of subsequent law and practice. In light of these factors, it appears likely that a constitutional challenge to a statute denying citizenship to persons born to unlawfully present or nonimmigrant aliens could possibly succeed in barring the statute, absent a constitutional amendment providing that such persons do not acquire citizenship by right of their birth in the United States.

End Notes

[1] *See generally, e.g.*, Dual Citizenship, Birthright Citizenship, and the Meaning of Sovereignty: Hearing Before the Subcomm. on Immigration, Border Security, and Claims of the H. Comm. on the Judiciary, 109th Cong. No. 63, at 2 (2005) ("2005 House Hearing"); Birthright Citizenship: Is It The Right Policy for America? Hearing before the Subcomm. on Immigration and Border Security of the House Committee on the Judiciary, 114th Cong., No. 21 (2015) ("2015 House Hearing").

[2] U.S. CONST. art. XIV, §1, cl. 1.

[3] *See, e.g.*, 2005 House Hearing, 2015 House Hearing, *supra* footnote 1. Note that a child born in the United States can sponsor a parent for eligibility for permanent residence in the United States only upon reaching the age of 21 and meeting various qualifications such as financial sponsorship; even with an eligible sponsor, unauthorized immigrants who entered the country without inspection may still be ineligible to adjust status. See Immigration and Nationality Act (INA) §§201(b)(2)(A)(i), 203, 213A, 245, 8 U.S.C. §§1151(b)(2)(A)(i), 1153, 1183a, 1255. However, the Obama Administration's proposal to create a new Deferred Action for Parental Accountability (DAPA) program would, if implemented, permit some alien parents of U.S. citizens or permanent residents to obtain temporary relief from removal. *See* U.S. Citizenship and Immigration Services, Executive Actions on Immigration (2015), http://www.uscis.gov/immigrationaction (describing proposal and noting federal court order barring implementation); CRS Legal Sidebar WSLG1273,

Implementation of DAPA and the DACA Expansion Remain Barred After Fifth Circuit Decision, by Kate M. Manuel.

[4] *See generally, e.g.*, 2005 House Hearing, *supra* footnote 1 (discussing case of Yaser Hamdi); *infra*, "*Hamdi v. Rumsfeld* and Presumption of Citizenship."

[5] *See, e.g.*, 2015 House Hearing, *supra* footnote 1; Oforji v. Ashcroft, 354 F.3d 609, 619-621 (7th Cir. 2003) (Posner, concurring).

[6] *E.g.*, Charles Wood, *Losing Control of America's Future – The Census, Birthright Citizenship, and Illegal Aliens*, 22 HARV. J. L. & PUB. POL'Y 465 (1999).

[7] For purposes of the Immigration and Nationality Act, the United States includes "Puerto Rico, Guam, the Virgin Islands of the United States, and the Commonwealth of the Northern Mariana Islands." 8 U.S.C. §1101(a)(38). The citizenship of children born on vessels in U.S. territorial waters or on the high seas has generally been held to be determined by the citizenship of the parents. Lam Mow v. Nagle, 24 F.2d 316 (9th Cir. 1928).

[8] *See generally infra*, "Litigation Involving the Citizenship Clause."

[9] Scott Bomboy, *What do other countries' constitutions say about birthright citizenship?*, CONSTITUTION DAILY (Aug. 26, 2015), http://blog.constitutioncenter.org/2015/08/what-do-other-countries-constitutions-say-about-birthrightcitizenship/ ("In general, birthright citizenship is common among Western Hemisphere countries and uncommon in other parts of the world.").

[10] *Id.*

[11] *See infra*, "Litigation Involving the Citizenship Clause."

[12] 112 U.S. 94 (1884).

[13] 169 U.S. 649 (1898).

[14] Indian Citizenship Act, P.L. 68-175, 43 Stat. 253 (1924); Nationality Act of 1940, P.L. 82-414, §201(b), 54 Stat. 1137, 1158; INA §301(b), 8 U.S.C. §1401(b)). The statutory expansion of automatic U.S. citizenship to Native Americans illustrates that the Citizenship Clause operates as a baseline guaranteeing the minimum of citizenship rights—wherever that baseline may be—and Congress has the power to provide citizenship to categories of people not covered by the constitutional guarantee. Congress has extended citizenship rights to children born of U.S. citizen parents in a foreign nation under certain circumstances. INA §301(c)-(e), (g), 8 U.S.C. §1401(c)-(e), (g).

[15] *See infra*, "Two Competing Interpretations of the Citizenship Clause."

[16] *See infra*, "Proposed Legislative Reinterpretations of the Citizenship Clause."

[17] INA §301(a), 8 U.S.C. §1401(a).

[18] *See, e.g.*, Walter Dellinger, Asst. Atty. Gen., *Legislation Denying Citizenship at Birth to Certain Children Born in the United States*, 19 OPS. OF THE OFFICE OF LEGAL COUNSEL 340, 348-349 (1995) (observing that "Congress is, of course, constitutionally free to propose, and the states to ratify, any amendment to the Constitution," but arguing that to do so would "tamper [with] ... basic presuppositions of American constitutionalism").

[19] *See infra*, "Two Competing Interpretations of the Citizenship Clause."

[20] U.S. CONST. art. I, §2, cl. 2 (Representatives); U.S. Const. art. I, §3, cl. 3 (Senators).

[21] U.S. CONST. art. II, §1, cl. 5.

[22] U.S. CONST. art. I, §8, cl. 4. Naturalization has been described by the Supreme Court as "the act of adopting a foreigner, and clothing him with the privileges of a native citizen." Boyd v. Nebraska *ex rel.* Thayer, 143 U.S. 135, 162 (1892).

[23] Act of March 26, 1790, 1 Stat. 103; Act of January 29, 1795, 1 Stat. 414; Act of April 14, 1802, 2 Stat. 153; Act of February 10, 1855, 10 Stat. 604. These naturalization acts specified that only "free white persons" could be naturalized.

[24] See "Common Law and the Constitution," in CRS Report R42097, *Qualifications for President and the "Natural Born" Citizenship Eligibility Requirement*, by Jack Maskell.

[25] Smith v. Alabama, 124 U.S. 465, 478 (1888). English common law was also often adopted or recognized as in force in the constitutions or early legislative actions of the original thirteen states. *See generally* Maskell, *supra* footnote 24.

[26] M'Creery's Lessee v. Somerville, 22 U.S. 354 (U.S. 1824).

[27] *See* Inglis v. Sailor's Snug Harbor, 28 U.S. (3 Peters) 99, 136 (1830) (Johnson, J., concurring) ("By the principles of [common] law, the demandant owed allegiance to the king of Great Britain, as of his province of New York. By the revolution that allegiance was transferred to the state ... [and thus the demandant] was entitled to inherit as a citizen, born of the state of New York."). *See also id.* at 164 (Story, J., dissenting in part on other grounds) ("Nothing is better settled at the common law than the doctrine that the children even of aliens born in a country, while the parents are resident there under the protection of the government, and owing a temporary allegiance thereto, are subjects by birth."). *See also, e.g.*, Murray v. The Schooner Charming Betsy, 6 U.S. (2 Cranch) 64, 119 (1804) (involving the claim of a person born in the United States, whom the Court presumed to be an American citizen in assessing whether he had expatriated or merely resided on a Danish island).

[28] Lynch v. Clarke, 1 Sandford Ch. 583, 646, 663 (N.Y. 1844) (concluding that "I can entertain no doubt, but that by the law of the United States, every person born within the dominions and allegiance of the United States, whatever were the situation of his parents, is a natural born citizen.").

[29] *Id.* at 656-663.

[30] *Id.* at 663.

[31] *See* U.S. CONST. art. 1, §2, cl. 3 (apportionment); *Elk v. Wilkins*, 112 U.S. 94 (1884).

[32] 60 U.S. 393, 411 (1857).

[33] *Id.* at 445-454.

[34] 14 Stat. 27, §1, 39 Cong. Ch. 31 (1866).

[35] *Id.*

[36] See Mark Shawhan, *"By Virtue of Being Born Here": Birthright Citizenship and the Civil Rights Act of 1866*, 15 HARV. LATINO L. REV. 1 (2012), for a presentation of some of the legislative history of the act pertaining to birthright citizenship principles. Much of the debate over the citizenship provision pertained to whether and to what extent Native Americans should be included or excluded.

[37] CONG. GLOBE, 39th Cong., 1st Sess. 498 (1866).

[38] *Id.*

[39] *Id.*

[40] *See id.*

[41] *Id.* at 527, 572.

[42] H.R. 127, 39th Cong. (1866); Cong. Globe, 39th Cong., 1st Sess. 2764 (1866).

[43] CONG. GLOBE, 39th Cong., 1st Sess. 2768 (1866).

[44] *Id.* at 2769.

[45] *Id.* at 2890.

[46] *Id.* Senator Howard continued, rather optimistically: "It settles the great question of citizenship and removes all doubt as to what persons are or are not citizens of the United States." *Id.*

[47] *Id.* at 2890-91. Senator Cowen was also, again, concerned with "the Gypsies," saying: "If the mere fact of being born in the country confers that right [to be shielded from expulsion by a state], then they will have it; and I think it will be mischievous." *Id.* at 2891.

[48] *Id.* at 2891.

[49] *See id.* at 2892-97.

[50] *Id.* at 2893.

[51] 16 Stat. 254 (1870); 10 Stat. 604 (1855).

[52] 83 U.S. (16 Wall.) 36 (1873).

[53] Craigmiles v. Giles, 110 F. Supp. 2d 658, 665 (E.D. Tenn. 2000).

[54] 83 U.S. at 74-79.

[55] *Id.* at 73.

[56] *See, e.g.*, United States v. Wong Kim Ark, 169 U.S. 649, 679 (1898); Brief of Amicus Curiae the Claremont Inst. Ctr. for Constitutional Jurisprudence in Supp. of Resp'ts. at 8-9, Hamdi v. Rumsfeld, 542 U.S. 507 (2004) (No. 03-6696).

[57] Elk v. Wilkins, 112 U.S. 94 (1884).

[58] *Id.* at 97.

[59] *Id.* at 109.

[60] *Id.* at 102. The Court also declared that the second section of the Fourteenth Amendment, which provides that "representatives shall be apportioned among the several States according to their respective numbers, counting the whole number of persons in each State, excluding Indians not taxed," supported the exclusion of members of recognized Indian tribes from birthright citizenship. *Id.* As noted above, Native Americans now are citizens not by virtue of the Fourteenth Amendment but by various statutes as well as earlier treaties naturalizing specific tribes. *See supra* footnote 14.

[61] 169 U.S. 649 (1898).

[62] *Id.* at 652-653.

[63] *Id.* at 652.

[64] *Id.* at 653.

[65] *Id.* at 649, 660, 666, 676-682.

[66] *See generally* Lucy E. Salyer, Wong Kim Ark, *in* IMMIGRATION STORIES 51, 70-74 (2005).

[67] 169 U.S. at 653-675.

[68] *Id.* at 654-666, 683-688.

[69] *Id.* at 675-676, 688, 697-699.

[70] *Id.* at 692-697 (citing *In re* Look Tin Sing, 21 F. 905 (C.C.D. Cal. 1884), and other California district court decisions, as well as state supreme court decisions from Nevada (State v. Ah Chew, 16 Nev. 50 (1881)) and New Jersey (Benny v. O'Brien, 29 Vroom (58 N.J. Law) 36 (1895))).

[71] *Id.* at 688-692.

[72] *Id.* at 676-682.

[73] *Id.* at 693.

[74] *Id.* at 693-694. The Court also observed that "[t]o hold that the Fourteenth Amendment of the Constitution excludes from citizenship the children, born in the United States, of citizens or subjects of other countries, would be to deny citizenship to thousands of persons of English, Scotch, Irish, German or other European parentage, who have always been considered and treated as citizens of the United States." *Id.* at 694.

[75] *E.g.*, *id.* at 657-658, 664, 678-679, 682, 688.

[76] *Id.* at 703.

[77] *Id.* at 705.

[78] *Id.*at 706-732. The core dissent argument—reflected in the modern legal debate over birthright citizenship—was that "to be 'completely subject' to the political jurisdiction of the United States is to be in no respect or degree subject to the political jurisdiction of any other government," and that:

The children of aliens, whose parents have not only not renounced their allegiance to their native country, but are forbidden by its system of government, as well as by its positive laws, from doing so, and are not permitted to acquire another citizenship by the laws of the country into which they come, must necessarily remain themselves subject to the same sovereignty as their parents, and cannot, in the nature of things, be, any more than their parents, completely subject to the jurisdiction of such other country.

Id. at 725.

[79] *Id.* at 725-732.

[80] *See supra* footnote 14.

[81] Children born to foreign diplomatic officers accredited to the United States may be considered lawful permanent residents at birth. 8 C.F.R. §101.3. *See also supra* footnote 7.

[82] *See, e.g.*, Perkins v. Elg, 307 U.S. 325, 328-329 (1939) ("On her birth in New York, the plaintiff became a citizen of the United States") (citing Civil Rights Act of 1866, Citizenship Clause, and *Wong Kim Ark*); Bedoya Lopez de Zea v. Holder, 761 F.3d 75, 78 (1st Cir. 2014) (noting that petitioner's child "is a United States citizen and was born ... during one of [petitioner's] visits to the United States," but upholding petitioner's removal); Hernandez-Rivera v. Immigration & Naturalization Service, 630 F.2d 1352, 1356 (9th Cir. 1980) (affirming rule disallowing minor U.S. citizen children from petitioning for their parents until age 21, noting "[a]n alien cannot gain favored status merely because he or she has a child who is a United States citizen").

[83] Regan v. King, 134 F.2d 413 (9th Cir. 1943).

[84] *Id.* at 413.

[85] 319 U.S. 753 (1943) (denying certiorari). *See also* Greg Robinson, "Regan v. King," DENSHO ENCYCLOPEDIA (Brian Niiya, ed.), http://encyclopedia.densho.org/Regan_v._King/ (last visited October 6, 2015).

[86] 457 U.S. 202 (U.S. 1982).

[87] *Id.* at 211 (emphasis in original).

[88] *Id.* at 213.

[89] *Id.* at 211 n.10 (citing C. BOUVE, EXCLUSION AND EXPULSION OF ALIENS IN THE UNITED STATES 425-427 (1912)).

[90] *Id.* at 219-220.

[91] Hamdi v. Rumsfeld, 542 U.S. 507 (2004).

[92] *Hamdi*, 542 U.S. at 507. Four separate opinions were written by the *Hamdi* Court, with none receiving support from a majority of the Justices. However, a majority of the Court recognized that Congress's enactment of the 2001 Authorization for Use of Military Force authorized the President to detain persons captured while fighting U.S. forces in Afghanistan, including U.S. citizens. *Id.* at 518 (O'Connor, J., plurality opinion), 588-589 (Thomas, J., dissenting). A clear majority also believed that U.S. citizens held as "enemy combatants" have the right to a hearing where they may challenge the legality of their detention before a judge or other neutral decision-maker. *Id.* at 518, 533 (O'Connor, J., plurality opinion, joined by Breyer, J., Kennedy, J., and Rehnquist, C.J.); 553 (Souter, J., concurring in part and dissenting in part, joined by Ginsburg, J.). Justices Scalia and Stevens took the view that detention without criminal charge was only permissible if

Congress suspended the writ of habeas corpus. *Id.* at 554 (Scalia, J., dissenting, joined by Stevens, J.).

93 Brief of Amicus Curiae Eagle Forum Education & Legal Defense Fund in Supp. of Resp'ts, Hamdi v. Rumsfeld, 542 U.S. 507 (2004) (No. 03-6696) (hereinafter "Eagle Forum Brief").

94 Brief of Amicus Curiae the Claremont Inst. Ctr. for Constitutional Jurisprudence in Supp. of Resp'ts., Hamdi v. Rumsfeld, 542 U.S. 507 (2004) (No. 03-6696) (hereinafter "Claremont Institute Brief").

95 Eagle Forum Brief at 4-13; Claremont Institute Brief at 5-19.

96 542 U.S. at 554 (Scalia, J., dissenting).

97 *See, e.g.*, Nolos v. Holder, 611 F.3d 279, 284 (5th Cir. 2010) (holding that persons born in the Philippines during its status as a U.S. territory were not "born ... in the United States" under the Fourteenth Amendment and distinguishing *Wong Kim Ark*); Valmonte v. INS, 136 F.3d 914, 915-21 (2d Cir. 1998) (same); Rabang v. INS, 35 F.3d 1449, 1450-54 (9th Cir. 1994) (same). Note that Congress has extended citizenship by statute to persons born in the current U.S. territories, except for American Samoa; citizenship was never extended to Filipinos before Philippine independence. *See* INA §101(a)(36), (38), 8 U.S.C. §1101(a)(36), (38). Thus, case law on this particular question mostly concerns American Samoa and the Philippines.

98 Tuaua v. United States, 788 F.3d 300 (D.C. Cir. 2015).

99 *Id.* at 304-306 (discussing United States v. Wong Kim Ark, 169 U.S. 649 (1898)).

100 *Id.* at 305-306 (discussing Elk v. Wilkins, 112 U.S. 94 (1884)).

101 *Id.* at 306-312. As summarized by Chief Justice Rehnquist in *United States v. Verdugo-Urquidez*, 494 U.S. 259, 268 (1990), "not every constitutional provision applies to governmental activity even where the United States has sovereign power." *See, e. g.*, Balzac v. Porto Rico, 258 U.S. 298 (1922) (Sixth Amendment right to jury trial inapplicable in Puerto Rico); Ocampo v. United States, 234 U.S. 91 (1914) (Fifth Amendment grand jury provision inapplicable in Philippines); Downes v. Bidwell, 182 U.S. 244 (1901) (Revenue Clauses of Constitution inapplicable to Puerto Rico).

102 Tuaua v. United States, 788 F.3d 300, 303 (D.C. Cir. 2015) (some citations omitted).

103 This is separate from the debate over whether a new amendment should be made to the Constitution to eliminate the automatic granting of U.S. citizenship to children of unlawfully or temporarily present aliens. However, some of those who believe that the Citizenship Clause already allows that result have also expressed support for such an amendment, if the prevailing interpretation of the Citizenship Clause is held to be required by its current text. *See, e.g.*, Wood, *supra* footnote 6, at 522; *Societal and Legal Issues Surrounding Children Born in the U.S. to Illegal Alien Parents: Joint Hearing before the Subcomm. on Immigration and Claims and the Subcomm. on the Constitution of the House Committee on the Judiciary*, 104th Cong. (1995).

104 *See* United States v. Wong Kim Ark, 169 U.S. 649, 683-686 (1898) (analyzing The Schooner Exchange v. McFaddon, 11 U.S. (7 Cranch) 116 (1812)); *see also, e.g.*, Dellinger, *supra* footnote 18; Robert E. Mensel, *Jurisdiction in Nineteenth Century International Law and its Meaning in the Citizenship Clause of the Fourteenth Amendment*, 32 ST. LOUIS U. PUB. L. REV. 329 (2013).

105 *See generally, e.g.*, PETER H. SCHUCK AND ROGERS M. SMITH, CITIZENSHIP WITHOUT CONSENT: ILLEGAL ALIENS IN THE AMERICAN POLITY (Yale University Press, 1985).

106 Note that different reinterpretations are aimed at different concerns. Some would exclude from automatic U.S. citizenship those born to non-domiciled temporary visitors (whether legally

present or not), but not unlawfully present aliens. *See, e.g.*, Richard Posner, *The Controversy over Birthright Citizenship*, THE BECKER POSNER BLOG (Oct. 17, 2010), http://www.becker-posner-blog.com/2010/10/the-controversy-over-birthright-citizenshipposner.html. Others would exclude those born to unlawfully present aliens, but not necessarily to those lawfully present, even temporarily as nonimmigrants. *See, e.g.*, Wood, *supra* footnote 6; Justin Lollman, *Note: The Significance of Parental Domicile Under the Citizenship Clause*, 101 VA. L. REV. 455 (2015). Still others propose that the Citizenship Clause does not require granting automatic U.S. citizenship to anyone but those with one or even both parents who are citizens or lawfully present and domiciled immigrants. *E.g.*, SCHUCK AND SMITH, *supra* footnote 105; *infra*, "Proposed Legislative Reinterpretations of the Citizenship Clause."

107 SCHUCK AND SMITH, *supra* footnote 105, at 86.

108 *See, e.g.*, Wood, *supra* footnote 6, at 506-508.

109 *See, e.g.*, Dellinger, *supra* footnote 18, at 346. The pro-reinterpretation view has also been called the "revisionist" approach, primarily by opponents. *See, e.g.*, Mark Shawhan, *"By Virtue of Being Born Here": Birthright Citizenship and the Civil Rights Act of 1866*, 15 HARV. LATINO L. REV. 1, 1-2 (2012).

110 Eagle Forum Brief, *supra* footnote 93, at 4. *See also supra*, "*Hamdi v. Rumsfeld* and Presumption of Citizenship."

111 *See, e.g.*, Lauren Carroll, *'Many' scholars say 'anchor babies' aren't covered by Constitution*, POLITIFACT.COM (Aug. 25, 2015), http://www.politifact.com/truth-o-meter/statements/2015/aug/25/donald-trump/trump-many-scholarssay-anchor-babies-arent-covere/ (quoting Peter Schuck that "our [consensualist] view on the constitutional issue is decidedly the minority view").

112 *E.g.*, Dan Stein and Jon Bauer, *Interpreting the 14th Amendment: Automatic Citizenship for Children of Illegal Immigrants?* , 7 STANFORD L. & POL'Y REV. 127, 128-129 (1996) (citing Lord Edward Coke, *Calvin's Case* (1608)); Wood, *supra* footnote 6, at 508-508 (same); *see also, e.g.*, SCHUCK AND SMITH, *supra* footnote 105, at 42("American law has in fact embodied ascriptive and consensual elements from its earliest days.").

113 *E.g.*, Lino A. Graglia, *Birthright Citizenship for Children of Illegal Aliens: An Irrational Public Policy*, 14 TEX.
REV. LAW & POL. 1, 10 (2009); Claremont Institute Brief, *supra* footnote 94, at 16-19; *see also* United States v. Wong Kim Ark, 169 U.S. 649, 710 (1898) (Fuller, J., dissenting).

114 *E.g.*, SCHUCK AND SMITH, *supra* footnote 105, at 87.

115 *See, e.g.*, United States v. Wong Kim Ark, 169 U.S. 649, 657-658, 664, 678-679, 682, 688 (1898).

116 Afroyim v. Rusk, 387 U.S. 253, 267 (1967).

117 *E.g.*, Wood, *supra* footnote 6, at, 508-510 (analyzing statements of Senators Trumbull, Howard, and Williams, Cong. Globe, 39th Cong., 1st Sess. 2893-2897 (1866)); SCHUCK AND SMITH, *supra* footnote 105, at 81-83 (same); Eagle Forum Brief, *supra* footnote 93, at 6-7 (also citing Senator Cowen).

118 *E.g.*, SCHUCK AND SMITH, *supra* footnote 105, at 80.

119 *See generally* CONG. GLOBE, 39th Cong., 1st Sess. 2790-2794 (1866).

120 *See generally* Garrett Epps, *The Citizenship Clause: A "Legislative History,"* 60 AM. U.L . REV. 331, 334-35 (2010); United States v. Wong Kim Ark, 169 U U.S. 649 (1898); *supra*, "The Fourteenth Amendment to the U.S. Constitution."

121 *Compare, e.g.*, John C. Eastman, Legal M emorandum No. 18, From Feudalism to Consent: Rethinking Birthright Citizenship, The Heritage Foundation (2006), *available at*

http://www.heritage.org/research/reports/2006/03/fromfeudalism-to-consent-rethinking-birthright-citizenship (the Civil Rights Act of 1866 formulation "makes clear" that "any child born on U.S. soil to parents who were temporary visitors to this country and who, as a result of the foreign citizenship of the child's parents, remained a citizen or subject of the parents' home country was not entitled to claim the birthright citizenship," and the Fourteenth Amendment was not intended to be broader); *with* Epps, *supra* footnote 120, at 349-353 (rebutting Eastman's interpretation and observing that the act's sponsors considered children of Chinese subjects, born in the United States, "undoubtedly" citizens under the act). *See also, e.g.*, Shawhan, *supra* footnote 109 (describing and excerpting l egi sl ative debates and supporting prevailing view of birthright citizenship).

[122] *See, e.g.*, 2015 House Hearing, *supra* footnote 1, at 8-9, 22-27 (statement of Eastman, saying *Wong Kim Ark*'s holding was confined to automatic citizenship of children of "people who are here lawfully and permanently who we have recognized as having some extent of allegiance to the United States" and its broader language was mere dicta); *id.* at 33, 35-36 (statement of Lino T. Graglia, siding with *Wong Kim Ark* dissenting justices but arguing that the case did not address situation of unlawfully present parents).

[123] *See, e.g.*, Wood, *supra* footnote 6, at 511 ("[P]roponents of the prevailing view ... argue that because illegal aliens are not within one of the specific common law exceptions, the general territorial rule would apply to them.") (discussing Dellinger, *supra* footnote 18); John Eastman and Ediberto Roman, *Symposium: The U.S. Immigration Crises: Enemies at Our Gates or Lady Liberty's Huddled Masses?: Article: Debate on Birthright Citizenship*, 6 FIU L. REV. 293, 306 (2011) (statement of Ediberto Roman); 2015 House Hearing, *supra* footnote 1, at 73 (statement of J. Richard Cohen).

[124] *See generally, e.g.*, Eastman and Roman, *supra* footnote 123.

[125] *E.g.*, Dellinger, *supra* footnote 18, at 347; Gerard N. M agl iocca, *Indians and Invaders: The Citizenship Clause and Illegal Aliens*, 10 U. PA. J. CONST. L. 499, 513-514 (2008). *Cf., e.g.*, Eagle Forum Brief, *supra* footnote 93, at 7 ("Fundamental principles of statutory interpretation require that the term 'jurisdiction' be construed in the context of 'citizenship', which means far more than physical presence.").

[126] SCHUCK AND SMITH, *supra* footnote 105, at 92 (citing 18 Stat. 477 (1875) as "the first federal exclusion legislation ... [which] barred convicts and prostitutes").

[127] *Id.* at 129.

[128] *Id.* at 92.

[129] Graglia, *supra* footnote 113, at 5-6.

[130] 22 Stat. 58 (1882), 23 Stat. 115 (1884), 25 Stat. 476, 504 (1888), 27 Stat. 25 (1892), 28 Stat. 390 (1894).

[131] *See, e.g.*, J. Thomas Scharf, *The Farce of the Chinese Exclusion Laws*, THE NORTH AM. REV. (Vol. 166, Iss. 494, 1898), *available at* http://www.digitalhistory.uh.edu/disp_textbook.cfm?smtID=3&psid=4055 (presenting opinion of a former immigration inspector that "the immigration [from China] has continued in spite of legislation forbidding it").

[132] *E.g.*, Magliocca, *supra* footnote 125, at 513-514 (noting Act Prohibiting Importation of Slaves, 2 Stat. 426 (1807)).

[133] Epps, *supra* footnote 120, at 351-352, 356-357, 361.

[134] *E.g.*, H.R. 3605, 102nd Cong. (1991); *see also* 2015 House Hearing, *supra* footnote 1, at 58 (testimony of Jon Feere, Center for Immigration Studies) (noting legislation to limit birthright citizenship introduced in "nearly every Congress" since early 1990s).

[135] *E.g.*, H.J.Res. 87, 104th Cong. (1995).

[136] *Societal and Legal Issues Surrounding Children Born in the U.S. to Illegal Alien Parents: Joint Hearing before the Subcomm. on Immigration and Claims and the Subcomm. on the Constitution of the House Committee on the Judiciary*, 104th Cong. (1995) (discussing 104 H.R. 705; 104 H.R. 1363; 104 H.J.Res. 56; 104 H.J.Res. 64; 104 H.J.Res. 87; 104 H.J.Res. 88; and 104 H.J.Res. 93, 104th Cong. (1995)).

[137] 2005 House Hearing, *supra* footnote 1. A bill had been introduced in that Congress to give any child born in the United States "the same citizenship and immigration status at birth as the citizenship and immigration status of the child's mother." End Birth Citizenship to Illegal Aliens Act of 2006, H.R. 6294, 109th Cong. (2006). That provision would have directly conflicted with *Wong Kim Ark*, and its "status of the child's mother" language does not appear to have been used in any subsequent citizenship legislation.

[138] S. 45, H.R. 140, 114th Cong. (2015).

[139] 8 U.S.C. §1408 (defining "Nationals but not citizens of the United States at birth").

[140] S.Amdt. 284 to S.Amdt. 271 to S. 178, 114th Cong. (2015). S. 178 became P.L. 114-22.

[141] 2015 House Hearing, *supra* footnote 1.

[142] *See generally id.*

[143] *See, e.g.*, SCHUCK AND SMITH, *supra* footnote 105, at 129; Eastman, *supra* footnote 121; 2015 House Hearing, *supra* footnote 1, at 28 (statement of John C. Eastman).

[144] *See, e.g.*, Editorial, *Born in the U.S.A.: A Primer on Birthright Citizenship and the U.S. Constitution*, WALL ST. J., Aug. 20, 2015, http://www.wsj.com/articles/born-in-the-u-s-a-1440113798; James C. Ho, Commentary: *Ban on Birthright Citizenship Unconstitutional*, WASH. TIMES Apr. 8, 2011, http://www.washingtontimes.com/news/2011/ apr/8/ban-on-birthright-citizenship-unconstitutional/; Saby Ghoshray, Rescuing the Citizenship Clause from Nativistic Distortion: A Reconstructionist Interpretation of the Fourteenth Amendment, 51 Washburn L.J. 261 (2012); Dellinger, *supra* footnote 18.

[145] Some, including a standing Department of Justice Office of Legal Counsel (OLC) Opinion from 1995, have argued that while a constitutional amendment to limit birthright citizenship would be within Congress's and the states' "naked power," it would violate "bedrock principles" of American constitutionalism relating to equality and other values. Walter Dellinger, Asst. Atty. Gen., *Legislation Denying Citizenship at Birth to Certain Children Born in the United States*, 19 OPS. OF THE OFFICE OF LEGAL COUNSEL 340, 348-349 (1995); *see also, e.g.*, "How Would the Constitution Change If We Abandoned the Birthplace Criterion?" in Christopher L. Eisgruber, *Birthright Citizenship and the Constitution*, 72 N.Y.U.L. REV. 54, 85-96 (1997).

[146] Kimel v. Fla. Bd. of Regents, 528 U.S. 62, 81 (2000) ("The ultimate interpretation and determination of the Fourteenth Amendment's substantive meaning remains the province of the Judicial Branch.").

[147] *See, e.g.*, City of Boerne v. Flores, 521 U.S. 507, 519 (1997) ("Congress does not enforce a constitutional right by changing what the right is. It has been given the power 'to enforce,' not the power to determine what constitutes a constitutional violation. Were it not so, what Congress would be enforcing would no longer be, in any meaningful sense, the 'provisions of [the Fourteenth Amendment].'"); *cf.* 2015 House Hearing, *supra* footnote 1, at 28 (testimony of Dr. John C. Eastman).

[148] Oforji v. Ashcroft, 354 F.3d 609, 621 (7th Cir. 2003) (Posner, concurring) (citing SCHUCK & SMITH, *supra* footnote 105, at 116-117, and Dan Stein & John Bauer, *Interpreting the 14th Amendment: Automatic Citizenship for Children of Illegal Immigrants*, 7 STANFORD L. & POLICY REV. 127, 130 (1996)). *Oforji v. Ashcroft* upheld a denial of derivative asylum for a Nigerian citizen on behalf of her U.S. citizen children; the citizenship of the children was

not questioned by the majority. *Id.* at 614-619. *See also* Richard Posner, *The Controversy over Birthright Citizenship*, THE BECKER POSNER BLOG (Oct. 17, 2010), http://www.becker-posner-blog.com/2010/10/the-controversy-over-birthright-citizenshipposner.html (stating potentially modified view that a constitutional amendment would "maybe not" be required to "clos[e] the loophole that encourages foreigners to come to the United States solely to make their future children U.S. citizens," but otherwise observing that "[c]oncern with birthright citizenship is probably misplaced").

149 *See, e.g.*, 2015 House Hearing, *supra* footnote 1, at 9, 33, 59-60 (statements of Dr. John C. Eastman, Professor Lino A. Graglia, and Jon Feere).

150 *E.g.*, Dellinger, *supra* footnote 18 (asserting that legislation denying automatic citizenship to persons born in the United States to parents who are not citizens or permanent resident aliens is "unquestionably unconstitutional"); 2015 House Hearing, *supra* footnote 1, at 74 (statement of J. Richard Cohen).

151 Matt Ford, *Could Birthright Citizenship Be Undone?*, THE ATLANTIC (Aug. 19, 2015), http://www.theatlantic.com/politics/archive/2015/08/could-birthright-citizenship-be-undone/401759/.

152 *See* Dellinger, *supra* footnote 18, at 349 ("permanent caste of aliens, generation after generation"); Epps, *supra* footnote 120, at 334.

153 Ford, *supra* footnote 151.

154 Wood, *supra* footnote 6.

155 Montejo v. Louisiana, 556 U.S. 778, 792-793 (2009).

156 Michigan v. Bay Mills Indian Cmty., 134 S. Ct. 2024, 2036 (2014).

157 Cohens v. Virginia, 9 U.S. 264, 399 (1821); *see* Meese/Eastman Brief at 14 (arguing that *Wong Kim Ark* "need not be read so expansively").

158 *See, e.g., supra*, '*Plyler v. Doe* and "Jurisdiction"'; Wood, *supra* footnote 6, at 519-521 (discussing and rejecting argument that the Citizenship Clause's jurisdiction requirement is the same as that under Equal Protection).

159 Afroyim v. Rusk, 387 U.S. 253, 267-268 (1967). *See also* Vance v. Terrazas, 444 U.S. 252, 260 (1980) (holding that the United States may not deprive a person "born or naturalized in the United States" of his U.S. citizenship "'unless he voluntarily relinquishes it.'" (quoting Afroyim, 387 U.S. at 262)); Jolley v. INS, 441 F.2d 1245, 1248 (5th Cir. 1971) ("[B]ecause of the precious nature of citizenship, it can be relinquished only voluntarily, and not by legislative fiat.").

160 *See supra*, "Proposed Legislative Reinterpretations of the Citizenship Clause" (discussing S. 45 and H.R. 140, 114th Cong. (2015)); *see also* 2015 House Hearing, *supra* footnote 1, at 28 (testimony of Dr. John C. Eastman urging Congress to clarify in those bills that "this retroactive grant of citizenship to people who were not 'subject to the jurisdiction' of the United States at the time of their birth ... is made pursuant to Congress's plenary power over naturalization, not because of some perceived mandate of the Fourteenth Amendment"). Note that as a matter of statutory construction, statutes are generally presumed to operate prospectively unless retroactivity is expressly indicated. Landgraf v. USI Film Prods., 511 U.S. 244, 265 (1994) ("[T]he presumption against retroactive legislation is deeply rooted in [this country's] jurisprudence, and embodies a legal doctrine centuries older than [the] Republic.").

In: Birthright Citizenship …
Editor: Garrett Manning
ISBN: 978-1-63485-258-6

Chapter 2

BIRTHRIGHT CITIZENSHIP UNDER THE 14TH AMENDMENT OF PERSONS BORN IN THE UNITED STATES TO ALIEN PARENTS*

Margaret Mikyung Lee

SUMMARY

Over the past couple of decades, growing concern about illegal immigration, chain migration, and national security has led some Members of Congress to reexamine the long-established tenet that a person who is born in the United States and subject to its jurisdiction is a citizen of the United States regardless of the race, ethnicity, or alienage of the parents. This concept of birthright citizenship is codified in the Citizenship Clause of the Fourteenth Amendment of the U.S. Constitution and Section 301(a) of the Immigration and Nationality Act (INA, codified at 8 U.S.C. §1401(a)). Proponents of birthright citizenship limits believe that the current law encourages illegal immigration by aliens hoping that their U.S.-born children will eventually enable lawful status for family members. The war on terror and the case of Yaser Esam Hamdi, a U.S.-Saudi dual national captured in Afghanistan fighting with Taliban forces, further heightened interest in restricting automatic birthright citizenship. Although Hamdi's parents were Saudi nationals in the United States on nonimmigrant work visas, Hamdi was a U.S. citizen by birth in Louisiana

* This is an edited, reformatted and augmented version of a Congressional Research Service, Publication No. RL33079, dated August 20, 2015.

and thus entitled to certain due-process rights not available to foreign enemy combatants. More recently, the media reports have drawn congressional attention to "birth tourism," in which wealthy, pregnant foreigners allegedly travel to the United States so that their children will be born as U.S. citizens. The 2016 presidential race renewed the debate on restricting automatic birthright citizenship due to Donald Trump's avowed support of restrictions followed by other candidates' statements supporting or opposing restrictions.

Consequent to these developments, in the 114th and recent Congresses, Members have introduced or supported bills that would revise or reinterpret the Citizenship Clause and/or the related citizenship statute. Some commentators assert that a constitutional amendment is required to restrict birthright citizenship, while others argue that a statutory interpretation of the Citizenship Clause would suffice. In the 114th Congress, H.R. 140 and S. 45 would amend the INA by interpreting "subject to the jurisdiction," text in the Citizenship Clause and the INA, to exclude from birthright citizenship persons born in the United States whose parents are unlawfully present in the United States or are nonimmigrant aliens. H.R. 2484 would restrict the admissibility of pregnant aliens who are seeking admission into the United States as B-visa/status tourists or short-term business visitors and, if admitted, are likely to give birth while in the United States.

Citizenship by birth in the United States was not defined in the original Constitution or in the early federal statutes. The states and courts in the United States apparently adopted the *jus soli* doctrine followed by traditional English common-law, under which persons born within the dominions of and with allegiance to the English sovereign are subjects of the sovereign regardless of the alienage status of their parents. The exceptions to this rule are persons born (1) to diplomats as subjects of the sovereign whom the parents represent abroad and (2) to citizens of a foreign, hostile occupying force as subjects of the invading sovereign. The doctrine's scope remained uncertain before enactment of the Civil Rights Act of 1866 and ratification of the Fourteenth Amendment in 1868.

These laws defined birthright citizenship, extending it to African Americans and also to most persons born in the United States. In an 1898 decision, *United States v. Wong Kim Ark*, the United States Supreme Court made clear that, under these laws, U.S.-born children of aliens were U.S. citizens regardless of the alienage and national origin of their parents, with narrow exceptions for the children of foreign diplomats and foreign, hostile occupation forces. In the 1884 decision *Elk v. Wilkins*, however, the Supreme Court held that Native Americans were not U.S. citizens under the terms of the Citizenship Clause. Native Americans were U.S. citizens by treaties or statutes granting U.S. citizenship to members of specific tribes. Immigration and nationality statutes enacted in 1924, 1940, and 1952 granted U.S. citizenship to all Native Americans.

INTRODUCTION

Over the past twenty-five years, concern about illegal immigration, chain migration, and national security has led some legislators to reexamine the long-established tenet of U.S. citizenship that a person, who is born in the United States and subject to its jurisdiction, is a citizen of the United States regardless of the race, ethnicity, or alienage of the parents. This concept of birthright citizenship is codified in the Citizenship Clause of the Fourteenth Amendment of the U.S. Constitution and §301(a) of the Immigration and Nationality Act (INA).[1] The war on terror and the case of Yaser Esam Hamdi, a U.S.-Saudi dual national captured in Afghanistan fighting with Taliban forces, further heightened attention to and interest in restricting automatic birthright citizenship. Although Hamdi's parents were Saudi nationals in the United States on nonimmigrant work visas, Hamdi was a U.S. citizen by right of his birth in Louisiana and arguably entitled to rights not available to foreign enemy combatants. More recently, the media reports have drawn congressional attention to "birth tourism," in which wealthy, pregnant foreigners allegedly travel to the United States so that their children will be born as U.S. citizens. The 2016 presidential race renewed the debate on restricting automatic birthright citizenship due to Donald Trump's avowed support of restrictions followed by other candidates' statements supporting or opposing restrictions. This report traces the history of birthright citizenship under U.S. law and discusses some of the legislation in recent Congresses intended to alter it.

In the current and recent Congresses, some Members have introduced or supported legislation that would revise or reinterpret the Citizenship Clause to address concerns that (1) children born to unauthorized aliens become an avenue to legal status for their parents and siblings when they turn 21 years old,[2] and (2) affluent pregnant foreigners come to the United States on tourist visas to give birth to their children and thus provide them with U.S. citizenship.[3] Such legislation also responds to more general public concern about the lack of movement on comprehensive federal immigration reform legislation.[4]

In the 114th Congress, H.R. 140 and S. 45 would amend the INA by interpreting "subject to the jurisdiction," text in the Citizenship Clause and the

INA, to exclude persons born in the United States from citizenship at birth if their parents were unlawfully present in the United States or were nonimmigrant aliens. In order for a child to be a citizen at birth under these proposals, at least one parent would have to be a U.S. national, a lawful permanent resident (LPR) who resides in the United States, or an alien serving on active duty in the U.S. Armed Forces. Also, H.R. 2484 would take a different approach to discouraging and preventing "birth tourism" by restricting the admissibility of pregnant aliens who are seeking admission into the United States as B-visa/status tourists or short-term business visitors and, if admitted, are likely to give birth while in the United States.No legislative action beyond committee referral has occurred on these measures.

Furthermore, some state legislators have voiced support for state legislation that would define state citizenship as excluding persons born to undocumented aliens and for a state compact under which states would issue a different type of birth certificate to such persons. Intending to set the stage for a U.S. Supreme Court review of the Citizenship Clause, state legislators from Arizona and 13 other states unveiled model legislation in January 2011.[5] Such legislation has been introduced in some states but has not been enacted.[6] Even if such legislation were enacted, some legal scholars think it is unlikely that the Supreme Court would hear such a case.[7] The prevalence of this type of legislation has diminished since 2011; such legislation apparently is pending only in New Jersey as of the date of this report.[8]

The American Bar Association (ABA), at its 2011 annual meeting, adopted a resolution urging Congress and state, territorial, and local legislative bodies to reject any revision of the 14th Amendment Citizenship Clause or any other attempt to restrict the ability of a person to claim U.S. citizenship under the 14th Amendment because of the citizenship or immigration status of the parents.[9]

HISTORICAL DEVELOPMENT

Jus Soli Doctrine before the Fourteenth Amendment

There are two basic doctrines for determining birthright citizenship. *Jus soli* is the principle that a person acquires citizenship in a nation by virtue of his birth in that nation or its territorial possessions.[10] *Jus sanguinis* is the principle that a person acquires the citizenship of his parents, "citizenship of the blood."[11] The English common law tradition prior to the Declaration of

Independence, which was the basis of the common law in the original 13 colonies and which was adopted by most of the states as the precedent for state common law,[12] followed the *jus soli* doctrine.[13] Persons born within the dominion of the sovereign and under the protection and ligeance of the sovereign were subjects of the sovereign and citizens of England; this included persons born to "aliens in amity" who owed temporary allegiance to the sovereign while in his territory.[14] The exceptions were persons born to members of a hostile occupying force or to diplomats representing another sovereign.[15] The reason was that the children of a hostile occupying force did not owe allegiance to nor were born under the protection of the proper sovereign of the occupied territory. The children of diplomats, although enjoying the temporary protection of the sovereign while in his/her dominions, actually owed allegiance to and had a claim to the protection of the sovereign whom their parents represented at the court of the sovereign in whose dominions they were born. All civilized nations recognize and assent to the immunity of foreign diplomats from their jurisdiction, without which a foreign ambassador might not be able to effectively represent the sending sovereign, but it would be "inconvenient and dangerous to society ... if [private individual aliens] did not owe temporary and local allegiance, and were not amenable to the jurisdiction of the country."[16]

The original framers of the U.S. Constitution did not define citizenship of the United States, although the Constitution required that a person have been a citizen of the United States for seven years to be a Representative and for nine years to be a Senator,[17] and that a person be a natural-born citizen or a citizen at the time of the adoption of the Constitution in order to be eligible to be President (and therefore, Vice President).[18] The Naturalization Act of 1790 and subsequent acts until the Civil Rights Act of 1866 and the ratification of the Fourteenth Amendment did not define citizenship by birth within the United States.[19] These naturalization acts specified that only free white persons could be naturalized. As a result of the absence of any definition in the Constitution or federal statutes of U.S. citizenship by birth in the United States, citizenship by birth in the United States generally was construed in the context of the English common law.[20] This provided the frame of reference and definition of "citizenship" that the framers of the Constitution would have understood and also provided the pre-independence precedent for state common laws. The acquisition of citizenship by birth and by naturalization in the United States depended on state laws, both statutory and common law, until the enactment of the naturalization law in 1790.[21] The Naturalization Act of 1790, enacted pursuant to the Congress's powers under the Constitution,[22] clearly established the definition of citizenship by naturalization, but Congress's silence on the issue of citizenship by birth in the United States caused some confusion and disagreement as to what the appropriate definition was. For example, some persons rejected the idea that English common law provided the proper rule for citizenship by birth in the United States.[23] And until the Civil War, some eminent jurists and legal scholars believed that there was no real citizenship of the United States separate from citizenship in a state; that is, a person was a citizen of a state which was part of the Union, therefore a person was a citizen of the United States by virtue of his citizenship in a state.[24]

Although the English common law at the time of the adoption of the Constitution considered a person born in the English dominions to alien parents to be an English citizen unless those alien parents fit into the exceptions described above, and although American law apparently generally accepted this position, there nevertheless appeared to be some uncertainty as to whether persons born in the United States to alien parents were, in fact, citizens of the United States. Some scholars ascribe this uncertainty to the desire of Americans to embrace both a "consensualist" doctrine of citizenship,[25] by which a person and a government consent to be mutually obligated, and an "ascriptive" doctrine by which a person is ascribed citizenship by virtue of circumstances beyond his control, such as birth within a particular territory or birth to parents with a particular citizenship.[26]

Apparently, *Lynch v. Clarke*, an 1844 New York case,[27] was the first case to decide the issue of whether the U.S.-born child of an alien was a U.S. citizen.[28] It held that the U.S.-born child of an Irish resident of the United States who returned to Ireland after the child's birth and died without ever declaring even an intent to be naturalized was a U.S. citizen. It held that the right of citizenship was a national right not pertaining to the individual states;[29] that state laws could no longer define U.S. citizenship;[30] and that national laws instead determined citizenship.[31] In determining the appropriate national law, the court rejected the consensualist doctrine in favor of the traditional English common-law doctrine of *jus soli*.[32] It rejected the argument that the application of the common-law doctrine was based on feudal principles inappropriate to the United States, which had been founded on the principles of consent between the government and the people to be governed, and found instead that the silence of the Constitution and the federal statutes indicated that Congress approved the adoption of the traditional common-law position.[33] The court also believed that even if federal laws did not indicate acquiescence in common-law doctrine, the common-law rule provided a well-defined, unambiguous, reliable rule without confusing recourse to the status of the parents.[34] It held that the national law defined any person born within the dominions and allegiance of the United States as a citizen, regardless of the status of the parents.[35] Notwithstanding the general acceptance of *jus soli*, in the minds of many persons, the issue of automatic citizenship upon birth in the United States to alien parents was still not to be decided definitively for many years, particularly where the parents were of a minority race or ethnicity.

Until the Civil Rights Act of 1866 and the Fourteenth Amendment, African Americans were not considered citizens of the United States. In the case of *Dred Scott v. Sandford*,[36] the United States Supreme Court held that African Americans could not be citizens of the United States, even if they were free, because they were descended from persons brought to the United States as slaves; the terms of the Constitution demonstrated that slaves were not considered a class of persons included in the political community as citizens;[37] and the various state laws indicated that African Americans had not been considered to be state citizens and that it was widely permitted to treat them as property at the time of the adoption of the federal Constitution.[38] The descendants of slaves could not have a citizenship right which their ancestors had not had upon the formation of the Union and which no law had subsequently granted them at the time of the *Dred Scott* decision.

The Fourteenth Amendment and the Civil Rights Act of 1866

The debates on the citizenship provisions of the Civil Rights Act of 1866 and the Fourteenth Amendment indicate that, although the primary aim was to secure citizenship for African Americans, these laws were intended to extend U.S. citizenship to all persons born in the United States and subject to its jurisdiction regardless of race, ethnicity or alienage of the parents.[39] The Civil Rights Act of 1866 declared that "all persons born in the United States and not subject to any foreign power, excluding Indians not taxed, are hereby declared to be citizens of the United States."[40] The Fourteenth Amendment declared that "[a]ll persons born or naturalized in the United States and subject to the jurisdiction thereof, are citizens of the United States and of the State wherein they reside."[41] The Civil Rights Act of 1866 differs from the Fourteenth Amendment by using the terms "not subject to any foreign power" and "excluding Indians not taxed."

During the debates on the Civil Rights Act of 1866, Senator Trumbull of Illinois, chairman of the committee that reported the bill, moved to amend it so that the first sentence read, "All persons born in the United States, and not subject to any foreign power, are hereby declared to be citizens of the United States without distinction of color."[42] Senator Cowan of Pennsylvania, who opposed both the Civil Rights Act of 1866 and the Fourteenth Amendment, asked "whether it will not have the effect of naturalizing the children of Chinese and Gypsies born in this country?" Senator Trumbull replied, "Undoubtedly." The two disagreed as to whether, under the law in existence prior to the enactment of the Civil Rights Act of 1866, Chinese Americans were citizens of the United States. Cowan raised the specter of unfettered Chinese immigration to California, resulting effectively in something tantamount to a takeover of California by the Chinese empire, if the proposed language were adopted. Trumbull asked Cowan whether the children born in Pennsylvania to German parents were not U.S. citizens, to which Cowan replied that Germans were not Chinese, Australians or Hottentots or the like. Trumbull replied that the law made no distinction between the children of Germans and Asiatics "and the child of an Asiatic is just as much a citizen as the child of a European."

Later in the debates, Senator Johnson of Maryland urged Senator Trumbull to delete the phrase "without distinction of color" because it was unnecessary since even without the phrase he understood that Trumbull's proposed amendment "comprehends all persons, without any reference to race or color, who may be so born."[43] Trumbull felt that it was better to retain the phrase to eliminate any doubt or dispute as to the meaning of his amendment.[44]

There was also a debate over whether Indians should be included or excluded from the citizenship provision. Trumbull believed that if the Indians were separated from their tribes and incorporated into the mainstream community then they already were U.S. citizens under the law.[45] Senator Lane of Kansas disagreed and felt that a more explicit bill was needed to extend citizenship to Indians, which he favored.[46] Other Senators wished to exclude Indians not taxed, which apparently was intended to exclude unassimilated Indians, who were deemed to be mostly living in an uncivilized condition in their tribes.[47] When the exclusion was adopted, Senator Henderson of Missouri objected that the citizenship of white persons did not depend on whether or not they were taxed and that it was unfair to make such a distinction for Indians, particularly since the issue of taxation was irrelevant to the issue of assimilation.[48]

During the debates on the Fourteenth Amendment, Senator Howard of Michigan moved to amend it by adding the first sentence in its present form, minus the phrase "or naturalized."[49] Senator Cowan again objected to language that he felt would include races such as the Chinese and prevent California from dealing with the massive Chinese immigrant population as it saw fit.[50] He again invoked the fear that California would be overrun by Chinese, Pennsylvania by Gypsies. He believed that the people of different races and cultures could not mingle. Senator Conness of California replied that he had supported the Civil Rights Act of 1866 and had no problem with constitutionally guaranteeing the U.S.-born children of Mongolian parents civil rights and equal protection, his support apparently influenced by his belief that the population of non-European immigrants and their descendants would not increase significantly.[51]

There was also debate as to whether Indians should be excluded from the scope of the Citizenship Clause of the Fourteenth Amendment and whether they were excluded by the phrase "subject to the jurisdiction thereof."[52] Apparently most of the Senators supported the idea of excluding Indians but disagreed as to whether the phrase "excluding Indians not taxed" should be inserted as it had been in the Civil Rights Act of 1866. Several Senators argued that "subject to the jurisdiction" meant the full and complete jurisdiction of the United States, and the Indians had always been considered subject to the jurisdiction of their tribes, which were quasi-foreign nations;[53] some also felt that the taxation requirement was problematic. Some Senators argued that "excluding Indians not taxed" was good enough for the Civil Rights Act so it was appropriate for the Fourteenth Amendment; they also argued that Indians were subject to U.S. jurisdiction for a variety of purposes so the "subject to the jurisdiction" language was insufficiently clear.[54] Ultimately, the Senate rejected the insertion of "excluding Indians not taxed," although at least one Senator said he voted against this insertion because he favored extending citizenship to Indians and not because he believed that the "subject to the jurisdiction language" excluded Indians already.[55]

United States v. Wong Kim Ark and Elk v. Wilkins

Despite the clarification in the debates that race, ethnicity, and alienage of parents would not affect the right to citizenship by birth in the United States, the issue concerning the meaning of the Civil Rights Act of 1866 and the Fourteenth Amendment was not settled until the 1898 case of *United States v. Wong Kim Ark*.[56] As the debates about those laws indicate, an underlying problem appears to have been the attitude that certain alien races and Native Americans/American Indians, like the African Americans in *Dred Scott*, could not be members of the American political community because they had not been members of the community that yielded the Declaration of Independence and the Constitution. The United States Supreme Court discussed the congressional debates described above, noting that although they were not admissible as evidence to control the meaning of the Fourteenth Amendment, they were important as an indication of the contemporaneous legal opinion of jurists and legislators and showed that Congress had explicitly considered the application of the Fourteenth Amendment to the Chinese (and other U.S.-born children of aliens).[57]

The Court traced the history of the statutory and common law regarding *jus soli* in England and America[58] and distinguished another case in which an alleged Chinese American had been found not to be a U.S. citizen, noting that the issue had been the insufficiency of proof that the claimant had been born in the United States.[59] But where birth in the United States was clear, a child of Chinese parents was, in the Court's opinion, definitely a citizen under the Fourteenth Amendment, even though Chinese aliens were ineligible to naturalize under then-existing law.[60] The Court rejected the argument that the child was born subject to the jurisdiction of the Chinese emperor and outside the jurisdiction of the United States because his allegiance and citizenship derived from his parents' remaining subjects to the Chinese emperor under treaties between the United States and China and the naturalization laws.[61] It noted and rejected the *Slaughter-House* Court's inaccurate statement that the exceptions to *jus soli* included the children of consuls and other aliens generally in addition to the children of ambassadorial-level diplomats and the children of hostile, occupying forces.[62] The decision alludes to a contemporaneous New Jersey case that held that a U.S.-born child of Scottish parents domiciled but not naturalized in the United States was born subject to the jurisdiction of the United States within the meaning of the Fourteenth Amendment and not subject to the jurisdiction of a foreign country within the meaning of the Civil Rights Act of 1866.[63] The Court held that the Fourteenth Amendment affirmed the traditional *jus soli* rule, including the exceptions of children born to foreign diplomats, to hostile occupying forces or on foreign public ships, and added a new exception of children of Indians owing direct allegiance to their tribes.[64] It further held that the "Fourteenth Amendment ... has conferred no authority upon Congress to restrict the effect of birth, declared by the Constitution to constitute a sufficient and complete right to citizenship"[65] and that it is "throughout affirmative and declaratory, intended to allay doubts and settle controversies which had arisen, and not to impose any new restrictions upon citizenship."[66]

Even after the Civil Rights Act of 1866, the Fourteenth Amendment and the *Wong Kim Ark* decision secured automatic birthright citizenship for all persons born in the United States and subject to its jurisdiction, Native American/American Indians s were not considered to be Fourteenth Amendment citizens because the U.S. Supreme Court determined that they were not born "subject to the jurisdiction" of the United States. Following earlier cases that had held that Indian tribes and their members were not subject to the jurisdiction of the United States, and language in the Constitution and the Civil Rights Act of 1866 that included only "Indians not taxed," the Court in Elk v. Wilkins[67] held that Indians were not citizens of the United States unless they had been naturalized by treaty or by a federal collective naturalization statute, or taxed or recognized as a citizen by the United States or a state. At the time of the decision, Native Americans/American Indians were not eligible to be naturalized on an individual basis according to the usual naturalization procedures and were only naturalized by treaty or statute.[68] The Court found that Native Americans/American Indians who had not been taxed or naturalized still owed immediate allegiance to the tribe and were members of an independent political community and thus were not subject to the jurisdiction of the United States and were not citizens of the United States.[69] The argument echoes those in the debates about the Fourteenth Amendment. John Elk had separated from his tribe and lived "under the jurisdiction of Nebraska" and had assimilated into mainstream society. Despite these facts, the Court held that he was not a U.S. citizen nor could he become one in the absence of treaty or federal statutory action regarding his tribe. Native Americans/American Indians are still not Fourteenth Amendment citizens;[70] they are citizens by virtue of one of the various statutes and treaties naturalizing specific tribes, the Citizenship Act of 1924 (which was ambiguous regarding those born after the act),[71] the Nationality Act of 1940 (which finally and unambiguously declared all Native Americans/American Indians born in the United States to be U.S. citizens),[72] or the Immigration and Nationality Act.[73]

LEGISLATIVE PROPOSALS

Constitutional and Statutory Amendments

In recent Congresses there have been various proposals aimed at excluding the children of unauthorized aliens and even nonimmigrant aliens from automatic birthright citizenship, partly to remove an incentive for aliens to enter the United States illegally, or enter legally on a nonimmigrant visa and then illegally stay beyond the visa period.[74] These proposals take the form of amendments to the Citizenship Clause of the Fourteenth Amendment or to the statutory provisions on birthright citizenship and comprise various approaches.[75] Although such proposals have been introduced in the 114th Congress, none of them have progressed beyond introduction.[76]

The legislation discussed in this section is intended to discourage unlawful entry and presence of aliens in the United States and the perceived anomaly of automatically granting citizenship to persons who, despite birth in the United States, are not raised and do not act in accordance with allegiance to the United States.[77] It may accomplish this but may also throw into question the ultimate status of many born here, that is, persons whose parents are in the United States initially on temporary visas but ultimately obtain lawful permanent status. Also, the additional record-keeping necessary to document who becomes a citizen automatically upon birth in the United States may present bureaucratic challenges, particularly since birth records are a matter for state laws.[78]

Constitutional Amendments and Related Statutory Amendments

Over the last couple of decades there have been several variations on proposals for constitutional amendments. The versions differ in defining what status a$_{7}$parent must have to enable automatic birthright citizenship for a child born in the United States. Proposals would variously limit *jus soli* citizenship under the Constitution to persons born to

- parents *both* of whom are either citizens or lawful permanent residents (does not expressly repeal the current Citizenship Clause);[80]
- a mother who is a legal resident (expressly repeals the current Citizenship Clause);[81]
- a mother who is a citizen or legal resident (expressly repeals the current Citizenship Clause);[82]
- parents one of whom is a citizen (does not expressly repeal the current Citizenship Clause);[83]
- parents one of whom is a citizen or person who owes permanent allegiance to the United States (does not expressly repeal the current Citizenship Clause);[84]

- parents one of whom is a legal resident (expressly repeals the current Citizenship Clause);[85]
- parents one of whom is a citizen or lawful permanent resident (does not expressly repeal the current Citizenship Clause);[86]
- parents one of whom is a citizen, is lawfully in the United States, or has lawful status under the immigration laws of the United States (does not expressly repeal the current Citizenship Clause);[87]
- parents one of whom is a citizen, a lawful permanent resident who resides in the United States, or an alien performing active duty service in the U.S. Armed Forces (does not expressly repeal the current Citizenship Clause).[88]

Even as a baseline for defining citizenship, some of the distinctions drawn are unclear. The term "legal resident" used in some of the proposals would appear to implicitly include citizens, nationals, and lawful permanent residents, but it may also be interpreted to include certain categories of nonimmigrants who typically reside in the United States for several years and other aliens permanently residing under the color of law. Other proposals refer to citizens, but not to nationals who are not citizens (e.g., American Samoans). One type of proposal refers to persons who owe permanent allegiance to the United States, which is how the INA defines nationals. Therefore, for the sake of clarity, proposed language that includes an explicit enumeration of the applicable categories of parents—citizens, nationals, lawful permanent residents, nonimmigrants (if any) may be preferable to language that only explicitly refers to parents who are legal residents or to citizens without mentioning nationals. Some proposals focus on the mother as the conduit for birthright citizenship, excluding a father who is a U.S. citizen or legal resident from being the conduit for such citizenship. All of these proposals would only apply prospectively to those born after the date of the ratification of an amendment by the legislatures of three-fourths of the states within seven years of its submission for ratification and several expressly provide that Congress shall have the power to enforce the article by appropriate legislation.

Some of the above proposals to amend the Constitution had or have parallel proposals to amend the INA to conform to the new baseline of the Citizenship Clause once it is amended, including, among others, legislation to limit citizenship by birth in the United States to persons born to

- mothers who are legal residents[89] or
- mothers who are citizens or legal residents.[90]

By their own terms, these types of statutory amendments would not take effect until a related constitutional amendment had been ratified and would only apply to those born after the date of ratification. These statutory proposals raise the same issues as the parallel constitutional amendments.

Statutory Amendments without Related Constitutional Amendments

One type of proposal would limit birthright citizenship in a way that its proponents believe would not necessitate a constitutional amendment (see discussion in the following section). It essentially would *statutorily* define persons born "subject to the jurisdiction" of the United States under the Citizenship Clause, notwithstanding the U.S. Supreme Court holdings in *United States v. Wong Kim Ark*. Proposals in this category variously define

- persons, whose birth mothers are not citizens, nationals, or lawful permanent residents of the United States *and* who are citizens/nationals of another country of which a natural parent is a citizen/national, as not being born subject to the jurisdiction of the United States within the meaning of the Fourteenth Amendment, but rather as being born subject to the jurisdiction of the other country;[91]
- persons, whose birth mothers are not citizens or lawful permanent residents of the United States *and* who are citizens/nationals of another country of which a natural parent is a citizen/national, as not being born subject to the jurisdiction of the United States within the meaning of the Fourteenth Amendment, but rather as being born subject to the jurisdiction of the other country;[92]
- persons born subject to the jurisdiction of the United States as including persons born *in wedlock* to a mother or father who is a U.S. citizen, a U.S. national, or a lawful permanent resident who maintains primary residence in the United States, or persons born *out of wedlock* to a mother who is a U.S. citizen, a U.S. national, or a lawful permanent resident who maintains primary residence in the United States;[93]
- persons born subject to the jurisdiction of the United States as including persons born *in wedlock* to a mother or father who is a U.S. citizen, a U.S. national, or a lawful permanent resident who maintains primary residence in the United States, or persons born *out of wedlock* to a mother who is a U.S. citizen, a U.S. national, or a lawful permanent resident who maintains primary residence in the United States, or to a father who is a U.S. citizen, a U.S. national, or a lawful

permanent resident who maintains primary residence in the United States, but only if paternity has been established by clear and convincing evidence and the father has satisfied certain requirements;[94]

- persons born subject to the jurisdiction of the United States as including persons born in the United States to a mother or father who is a national of the United States (this would include citizens and non-citizen nationals) or a lawful permanent resident who maintains his or her residence in the United States;[95]
- persons born subject to the jurisdiction of the United States as including persons born in the United States to a mother or father who is a citizen or national of the United States, a lawful permanent resident whose residence is in the United States, or an alien performing active duty service in the U.S. Armed Forces.[96]

The first two of these proposals would avoid the problem of rendering a person stateless by permitting persons born to unauthorized alien or nonimmigrant mothers to be citizens at birth if they have no viable claim to citizenship in another country.[97] These two proposals could result in a scenario in which a person may be born in the United States to a mother who is a nonimmigrant or unauthorized alien and a father who is a U.S. citizen, national or lawful permanent resident (in or out of wedlock) and not be born a U.S. citizen because that person has a claim to citizenship in the mother's country. The third proposal does not permit a person born out of wedlock to a father who is a U.S. citizen, national or lawful permanent resident to be considered born subject to the jurisdiction of the United States and does not provide for the acquisition of U.S. citizenship by such a person through a U.S. citizen father. Without conforming amendments to §309 of the INA, this proposal would mean that persons born abroad out of wedlock to a U.S. citizen father and an alien mother would have a process by which they could be deemed U.S. citizens at birth and, paradoxically, persons born in the United States of similar parentage would not. These proposals are all therefore arguably unconstitutional on due process/equal protection grounds as well as Citizenship Clause grounds.[98] The fourth proposal avoids such issues by providing for the birthright citizenship of a person born out-of-wedlock to a father who is a U.S. citizen, national, or lawful permanent resident as long as requirements like those of INA §309 are satisfied. The fifth and sixth proposals listed above would not raise these constitutional issues because they make no distinctions based on the gender of the parent.

Other Statutory Amendments

One type of proposal in the 110th and 109th Congresses, without statutorily defining "born subject to the jurisdiction" of the United States, would have provided that, with respect to a person born after the date of the enactment of the proposal, the person shall not be a national or citizen at birth under §301 of the INA (8 U.S.C. §1401) unless at least one of the parents is, at the time of birth, a citizen or national of the United States or an alien lawfully admitted for permanent residence.[99]

Last, a proposal in the 108th Congress was *sui generis*; it did not purport to be a congressional interpretation of the Citizenship Clause but would have imposed a statutory limitation on H-visa holders and therefore would have been unconstitutional under the Citizenship Clause. Under this proposal, children born to a parent who is a nonimmigrant employee under §101(a)(15)(H) of the INA would not be a U.S. citizen by birth in the United States unless the other parent were a U.S. citizen or lawful permanent resident.[100]

Congressional Act without Constitutional Amendment

Proponents of certain proposals to amend the INA argue that congressional interpretation of the Citizenship Clause to limit automatic birthright citizenship may be permissible without an accompanying constitutional amendment because, under §5 of the Fourteenth Amendment, Congress has the power to "enforce, by appropriate legislation, the provisions of this article."[101] In a still evolving area of law, the United States Supreme Court has held that Congress has some power to define the substance of the rights that are protected under the amendment and may even, under some circumstances, legislate contrary to judicial decisions by going beyond judicial decisions defining such rights in order to enforce the amendment.

In *Katzenbach v. Morgan*,[102] the Court found that Congress could define the substantive scope of equal protection for the purpose of determining whether state laws violate equal protection. The Court rejected the dissent's concern that Congress could legislate to dilute the equal protection and due process decisions of the Court, saying that Congress may adopt measures only to enforce Fourteenth Amendment rights, not to restrict, abrogate or dilute them.[104] However, Congress has passed legislation that purported to overrule the Court's expansion of the right against self-incrimination and the right-to-counsel and expressly relied on *Katzenbach v. Morgan*, although the Court, contemporaneously with the legislation, changed course to adopt a view in alignment with that of Congress.[105] Congressional abortion opponents have tried to initiate legislation restricting the right that the Court has derived from the Constitution.[106] Other more recent cases show that the Court will not always defer to Congress's determination as to what legislation is appropriate to enforce the provisions of the Fourteenth Amendment.[107]

Thus, there may be an issue as to whether Congress could define "subject to the jurisdiction thereof" in a manner that would curtail a long-assumed right of persons born to aliens in the United States to be U.S. citizens regardless of the immigration status of their parents. One could argue that Congress has no power to define "subject to the jurisdiction" and the terms of citizenship in a manner contrary to the Court's understanding of the Fourteenth Amendment as expressed in *Wong Kim Ark* and *Elk*, particularly since that understanding includes a holding that the Fourteenth Amendment did not confer on Congress a right to restrict the effect of birth on citizenship as declared by the Constitution. In other words, there may be a distinction between the existence of a right under the Fourteenth Amendment (e.g., citizenship), which depends on the text and judicial interpretation, and the implications or scope of the right, which is subject to some degree of congressional regulation. However, since Congress has broad power to pass necessary and proper legislation to regulate immigration and naturalization under the Constitution, Art. I, §8, cls. 4 & 18,[108] arguably Congress has the power to define "subject to the jurisdiction thereof" for the purpose of regulating immigration.

The federal courts arguably support an interpretation of the Constitution that would foil those who attempt to gain an immigration advantage by breaking U.S. laws, although *Wong Kim Ark* made no distinction between lawfully and unlawfully present alien parents, nor between legal resident and nonimmigrant aliens. However, the *Wong Kim Ark* Court did not have to make such distinctions, because Wong's parents were legal resident aliens. Federal appellate courts have upheld the refusal by the immigration enforcement authorities to stay the deportation of unauthorized aliens merely on the grounds that they have U.S.-citizen, minor children, because to do so would be unfairly to grant an advantage to aliens who successfully flouted U.S. immigration laws long enough to have a child born in the United States over those aliens who followed the law, and would turn the immigration statute on its head.[109] Although the mere fact of the existence of U.S.-citizen, minor children would not be sufficient to prevent the deportation of unauthorized alien parents, extreme hardship to the children caused by the deportation of the parents is a factor to be considered in the discretionary suspension of deportation.[110] The United States Supreme Court has upheld the discretion of the Attorney General and the immigration enforcement authorities to define "extreme hardship" under proceedings for the suspension of deportation[111] and to deny suspension of deportation and refuse to reopen proceedings for the suspension of deportation even if a prima facie case for suspension is demonstrated.[112] The Court held that a court could not substitute a liberal definition of "extreme hardship" for a narrow one preferred by the Attorney General and the immigration enforcement authorities, noting that otherwise "any foreign visitor who has fertility, money, and the ability to stay out of trouble with the police for seven years can change his status from that of tourist or student to that of permanent resident without the inconvenience of immigration quotas. This strategy is not fair to those waiting for a quota."[113] A U.S.-citizen child must be 21 years old to bring alien parents into the United States as immigrants.[114] Federal courts have found that this requirement is meant "to prevent wholesale circumvention of the immigration laws by persons who enter the country illegally and promptly have children to avoid deportation,"[115] and does not violate equal protection by distinguishing between U.S.-citizen children who are minors and those who have attained majority.[116]

The courts apparently have never ruled on the specific issues of whether the native-born child of unauthorized aliens as opposed to the child of lawfully present aliens may be a U.S. citizen or whether the native-born child of nonimmigrant aliens as opposed to legal permanent resident aliens may be a U.S. citizen.[117] However, *Wong Kim Ark* specifically held that, under the Fourteenth Amendment, a child born in the United States to parents who, at the time of his birth, were subjects of the Chinese emperor, but had a "permanent domicil [*sic*] and residence in the United States"[118] and were not diplomats of the emperor, was a U.S. citizen at birth. The holding does not make a distinction between illegal and legal presence in the United States, but one could argue that the holding is limited to construing the Fourteenth Amendment in the context of parents who are legal permanent residents. However, the Court's own discussion of the common law doctrine of *jus soli* and its affirmation by the Fourteenth Amendment indicates that the holding, at the least, would not be limited to permanent legal residents as opposed to nonimmigrant, transient, legal aliens.[119] Currently accepted law would also weigh against the argument that the Fourteenth Amendment limits citizenship to the children of lawful permanent residents.[120]

Furthermore, the cases involving the deportation of unauthorized aliens simply take for granted that their U.S.-born children are U.S. citizens in considering whether the existence of extreme hardship to U.S.-citizen, minor children should stay the deportation of the parents.[121] This is true regardless of whether the children were born during the period of any lawful stay by the parents, during the period of any unlawful stay, or after an immigration court's finding of deportability of the parents. However, some scholars argue that the Citizenship Clause of the Fourteenth Amendment should not apply to the children of unauthorized aliens because the problem of unauthorized aliens did not exist at the time the Fourteenth Amendment was considered in Congress and ratified by the states.[122]

Although the *Elk* decision construed the phrase, "subject to the jurisdiction thereof," the situation of Native Americans is unique, so any interpretation that the U.S.-born children of unauthorized aliens are not born "subject to the jurisdiction" of the United States arguably could not rely on the *Elk* decision.

Because of the Supreme Court interpretations of U.S. citizenship laws and constitutional provisions, one could argue that a constitutional amendment is necessary to clarify the meaning of "subject to the jurisdiction of the United States." On the other hand, *amicus curiae* (friend of the court) briefs submitted by several interested organizations to the U.S. Supreme Court for consideration during the case of *Hamdi v. Rumsfeld*[123] argued, among other things, that the Supreme Court interpretations never contemplated or intended to include the granting of automatic citizenship by birth in the United States to persons whose parents were aliens who entered or stayed in the United States unlawfully or who were transiently present. Notwithstanding such arguments, the Court itself made its decision in the *Hamdi* case based on the assumption that Hamdi was a U.S. citizen. Most other *jus soli* countries have limited citizenship by birth in their territories.[124]

End Notes

1 Codified at 8 U.S.C. §1401(a).

2 See, for example, 157 Cong. Rec. H3096 (daily ed. May 5, 2011) (statement of Rep. King).

3 See, for example, Daniel González, "Births by U.S. visitors: A real issue? Data indicate 'birth tourism' is not a widespread practice," *Arizona Republic*, August 17, 2011, http://www.azcentral.com/news/articles/2011/08/17/ 20110817births-by-us-visitors-smaller-issue.html; Rob Hotakainen, "'Birthright Citizenship' Will Be Target of House GOP Majority," *McClatchy Newspapers*, November 18, 2010, http://www.mcclatchydc.com/ 2010/11/18/103946/ birthright-citizenship-will-be.html#.

[4] J. Taylor Rushing and Bob Cusack, *GOP leader McConnell: Fourteenth Amendment is in need of review*, THE HILL, August 2, 2010; Miriam Jordan, Jean Guerrero, Laura Meckler, *U.S. Immigration Fight Widens to Native Born*, WALL ST. J., July 30, 2010, at A5.

[5] State Rep. Daryl Metcalfe, State Legislators for Legal Immigration, "State Lawmakers Convened in D.C. to Deliver Historic, Nationwide Correction of 14th Amendment Misapplication," January 5, 2011, http://www.statelegislatorsforlegalimmigration.com/NewsItem.aspx?NewsID=10195; *Associated Press*, "Lawmakers in 14 States Craft Bill to Deny Citizenship to 'Anchor Babies,'" October 19, 2010, listed the 13 other states as Alabama, Delaware, Idaho, Indiana, Michigan, Mississippi, Montana, Nebraska, New Hampshire, Oklahoma, Pennsylvania, Texas, and Utah, at http://www.foxnews.com/politics/2010/10/19/lawmakers-states-craft-denycitizenship-anchor-babies/?test=latestnews. Some legal scholars think it is unlikely the Supreme Court will hear such a case. Valeria Fernández, "Birthright Citizenship's Unlikely Road to Supreme Court," *New America Media*, December 22, 2010, http://newamericamedia.org/2010/12/birthright-citizenships-unlikely-road-to-supreme-court.php.

[6] For example, S.B. 1308, 50th Leg., 1st Reg. Sess. (Ariz. 2011), failed to pass in the State Senate on March 17, 2011. Other states have introduced legislation, *e.g.*, H.B. 1413, 117th Gen. Assemb., 1st Reg. Sess. (Ind. 2011); H.B. 1032, 2011 Reg. Sess. (Md. 2011); H.B. 2092, 53rd Leg., 1st Sess. (Okla. 2011); S.B. 897, 53rd Leg., 1st Sess. (Okla. 2011); H.B. 3207, 80th Leg. (W. Va. 2011). In Texas, a bill was introduced, not involving an interstate compact, to restrict issuance of a birth certificate to a child who had at least one parent who was a U.S. citizen, U.S. noncitizen national, or a lawful permanent resident residing in the United States; a temporary report of birth would be issued to other children. H.B. 292, 82nd Leg. (Tex. 2011).

[7] Valeria Fernández, "Birthright Citizenship's Unlikely Road to Supreme Court," *New America Media*, December 22, 2010, http://newamericamedia.org/2010/12/birthright-citizenships-unlikely-road-to-supreme-court.php, citing both scholars who believe interpretation of the Citizenship Clause has been settled to cover those born to unauthorized alien parents and those who believe it has not because prior cases did not expressly consider whether the Clause's scope included unauthorized alien parents. Both consider that any state law purporting to define federal, national citizenship would be unconstitutional.

[8] A3099, 216th Leg. (N.J. 2014).

[9] At its annual meeting in August 2011 ABA House of Delegates adopted resolution 303, available at www.abajournal.com/files/303.pdf; see also the report accompanying the resolution at http://lawprofessors.typepad.com/files/1312996198resolution303report.pdf, and, with other information, at http://www.abajournal.com/files/2011_hod_annual_meeting_303.authcheckdam_.pdf.

[10] Black's Law Dictionary 775 (10th Ed. 2014); entry for "jus soli" defines it as the "rule that a child's citizenship is determined by place of birth. This is the U.S. rule, as affirmed by the 14th Amendment to the Constitution."

[11] *Id.*; entry at "jus sanguinis" defines it as the "rule that a child's citizenship is determined by the parents' citizenship. Most countries follow this rule."

[12] *Lynch v. Clarke*, 1 Sandford Ch. 583, 646 (N.Y. 1844); 4 CHARLES GORDON, STANLEY MAILMAN & STEPHEN YALELOEHR, IMMIGRATION LAW AND PROCEDURE §92.03[1][b] (2015); Isidor Blum, *Is Gov. George Romney Eligible to be President? [part two]*, New York Law Journal, p. 1, col. 5 (October 17, 1967).

[13] 4 GORDON, MAILMAN & YALE-LOEHR, *supra* footnote 12, at §92.03[1][a & b]; Jill A. Pryor, *The Natural-Born Citizen Clause and Presidential Eligibility: An Approach for Resolving Two Hundred Years of Uncertainty*, 97 Yale L.J. 881, 886 & n. 24 (1988).

[14] *United States v. Wong Kim Ark*, 169 U.S. 649, 655-668 (1898); *Lynch v. Clarke*, 1 Sandford Ch. at 670; *Calvin's Case*, 7 Coke's Reports 1, 8-21 (1607)(as reprinted in vol. 4 of the 1826 edition edited by John H. Thomas & John F. Fraser).

[15] *United States v. Wong Kim Ark*, 169 U.S. at 675, 682-688; *Calvin's Case*, 7 Coke's Reports at 10-11.

[16] *United States v. Wong Kim Ark*, 169 U.S. at 683-688, citing the case of The Exchange, 7 Cranch. 116 (1812).

[17] U.S. Const. art. I, §2, cl. 2 (Representatives), U.S. Const. art. I, §3, cl. 3 (Senators).

[18] U.S. Const. art. II, §1, cl. 5.

[19] Act of March 26, 1790, 1 Stat. 103; Act of January 29, 1795, 1 Stat. 414; Act of April 14, 1802, 2 Stat. 153; Act of February 10, 1855, 10 Stat. 604.

[20] *Lynch v. Clarke*, 1 Sandford Ch. at 646, 658; Isidor Blum, *supra* footnote 12, at p. 1, col. 5.

[21] One should note that the determination of U.S. citizenship by naturalization also depended on state laws prior to the enactment of the first federal naturalization act. The election of Albert Gallatin to the U.S. Senate in 1793 was successfully challenged on the grounds that he had not been a U.S. citizen for nine years as required by the Constitution. 4 ANNALS OF CONGRESS, 3rd Cong. 47-55, 57-62 (Gales & Seaton 1849—there may be some difference in the pagination between different printings of the same congressional debates) (covering period of February 20-28, 1794). He claimed that he had become a citizen of either Virginia or Massachusetts at least nine years before his election. But a majority of the Senate, upon an examination of the Virginia and Massachusetts citizenship laws, decided that Gallatin had not satisfied the residency of either state prior to moving to Pennsylvania, where he ultimately settled and was elected to Congress. He had not been resident in Pennsylvania for nine years prior to election. This example also illustrates the pre-Constitution position that U.S. citizenship could not exist without state citizenship, which some legal scholars continued to espouse until the Civil War. Although Gallatin had resided in the United States for 13 years, he had not satisfied all the requirements for citizenship in the states where he had resided nine years before election. Gallatin tried to argue, *inter alia*, that U.S. citizenship was not dependent on state citizenship laws which had existed before independence because U.S. citizenship depended on allegiance to the new nation and even persons who had been natural-born citizens of the states were not considered citizens of the United States if they had not shown allegiance to the new government and nation.

[22] U.S. Const. art. I, §8, cls. 4 & 18.

[23] *See*, e.g., *Lynch v. Clarke*, 1 Sandford Ch. at 657; 4 GORDON, MAILMAN & YALE-LOEHR, *supra* footnote 12, at §92.03[1][b]. n. 9; PETER H. SCHUCK & ROGERS M. SMITH, CITIZENSHIP WITHOUT CONSENT: ILLEGAL ALIENS IN THE AMERICAN POLITY, 50-54 (1985).

[24] *Slaughter-House Cases*, 16 Wallace 36, 72 (1873); Leonard W. Levy, Kenneth L. Karst & Dennis J. Mahoney, *Citizenship (Historical Development)*, Encyclopedia of the American Constitution 258 (1986).

[25] Cases arose in the United States through the early nineteenth century concerning the issue of citizenship of natural-born state citizens whose allegiance to the United States was in question. Generally, such citizens had left the United States for England or English dominions before or during the Revolutionary War and no act by them or their home state had affirmed their allegiance to the independent state or the United States. Factors relevant

to this consensual citizenship included whether the person was born before or after July 4, 1776; whether the person left for England before or after July 4, 1776; whether the person was a minor at the time of departure for England; whether the person elected to affirm U.S. allegiance upon attaining majority; and whether the person was born or residing in territory during its occupation by the British on or after July 4, 1776. For example, if a person was born a British subject, i.e., before July 4, 1776, and as an adult did not adhere to the independent states after July 4, 1776, he remained a British subject. Generally, if he was born after July 4, 1776, he was a U.S. citizen, unless he was born in British-occupied territory, left for England as a minor, and did not elect to affirm his U.S. citizenship within a reasonable time after attaining his majority. *See Inglis v. Sailor's Snug Harbor*, 28 U.S. (3 Peters) 99 (1830). *But see McIlvaine v. Cox*, 8 U.S. (4 Cranch) 208 (1808), where the Court held that a person who joined the British Army and left for England still had inheritance rights because initially he had remained in New Jersey after July 4, 1776, and after New Jersey had passed legislation declaring itself an independent and sovereign state and its residents to be citizens of the independent state, and thus he had become a citizen of independent New Jersey. *See also Shanks v. Dupont*, 28 U.S. (3 Peters) 242 (1830), holding that a woman born in South Carolina before July 4, 1776, and remaining there afterward, was a citizen of independent South Carolina and her subsequent marriage to a British soldier during the occupation of her hometown did not change this status. However, her subsequent removal to England with her husband in 1782 rendered her a British subject within the meaning of the treaty of 1794 which recognized inheritance rights for British subjects with property in the United States. For a discussion of case law, legislative history of the Fourteenth Amendment, and a theory of citizenship based on fairness, reciprocity, and consent, see William Ty Mayton, *Birthright Citizenship And The Civic Minimum*, 22 Geo. Immigr. L.J. 221 (2008) (arguing that fairness dictated that the children of lawfully present aliens should be birthright citizens under the Citizenship Clause, but did not dictate that children of unlawfully present aliens must be birthright citizens).

[26] SCHUCK & SMITH, *supra* footnote 23, at 42-62.

[27] 1 Sandford Ch. 583

[28] SCHUCK & SMITH, *supra* footnote 23, at 57.

[29] 1 Sanford Ch. at 641.

[30] 1 Sanford Ch. at 643-5.

[31] *Id.*

[32] 1 Sandford Ch. at 656-663.

[33] *Id.*

[34] 1 Sandford Ch. at 658.

[35] 1 Sandford Ch. at 663.

[36] 60 U.S. (19 How.) 393 (1856).

[37] 60 U.S. (19 How.) at 411.

[38] 60 U.S. (19 How.) at 407-416.

[39] For additional analyses of the legislative history of the Fourteenth Amendment's Citizenship Clause, see *Birthright Citizenship: Is It The Right Policy For America?, Hearing Before the Subcommittee on Immigration and Border Security of the Committee on the Judiciary, House of Representatives*, Serial No. 114-21, 114th Cong. (2015) (hereinafter *Birthright Citizenship Hearing*); testimony of witnesses representing opposing positions at the *Joint Hearing Before the Subcommittee on Immigration and Claims and the Subcommittee on the Constitution of the Committee on the Judiciary, House of Representatives*, Serial No. 50, 104th Cong. (1995) (hereinafter *Joint Hearing*); see also, Garrett Epps, *The Citizenship*

Clause: A "Legislative History," (June 20, 2010), available at Social Science Research Network website, http://ssrn.com/abstract=1627665; James C. Ho, *Defining "American": Birthright Citizenship and the Original Understanding of the 14th Amendment*, and Elizabeth B. Wydra, *Debunking Modern Arguments Against Birthright Citizenship*, in Immigration Policy Center, *Made in America: Myths & Facts About Birthright Citizenship* (September 2009); Charles Wood, *Losing Control of America's Future: the Census, Birthright Citizenship, and Illegal Aliens*, 22 Harv. J. L. & Pub. Pol'y 465, 504-519 (1999); Christopher L. Eisgruber, *Birthright Citizenship and the Constitution*, 2 N.Y.U.L. Rev. 54 (1997).

[40] C. 31, §1, 14 Stat. 27.

[41] Ratified July 9, 1868.

[42] Cong. Globe, 39th Cong., 1st Sess. 498 (1866). The quotations from the colloquy described in this paragraph are all located at this citation.

[43] Cong. Globe, 39th Cong., 1st Sess. 573-574 (1866).

[44] *Id.*

[45] Cong. Globe, 39th Cong., 1st Sess. 498-499 (1866).

[46] *Id.*

[47] Cong. Globe, 39th Cong., 1st Sess. 571-573 (1866).

[48] Cong. Globe, 39th Cong., 1st Sess. 571 (1866).

[49] Cong. Globe, 39th Cong., 1st Sess. 2890 (1866).

[50] Cong. Globe, 39th Cong., 1st Sess. 2890-2891 (1866).

[51] Cong. Globe, 39th Cong., 1st Sess. 2891-2892 (1866).

[52] Cong. Globe, 39th Cong., 1st Sess. 2890-2897 (1866).

[53] Cong. Globe, 39th Cong., 1st Sess. 2890, 2893, 2895, 2897 (1866) (remarks of Senator Howard of Michigan, Senator Trumbull of Illinois, Senator Williams of Oregon).

[54] Cong. Globe, 39th Cong., 1st Sess. 2892, 2893, 2895 (1866) (remarks of Senator Doolittle of Wisconsin, Senator Johnson of Maryland, Senator Hendricks of Indiana).

[55] Cong. Globe, 39th Cong., 1st Sess. 2897 (1866) (remarks of Senator Saulsbury of Delaware).

[56] 169 U.S. 649 (1898).

[57] 169 U.S. at 697-699.

[58] 169 U.S. at 655-675.

[59] 169 U.S. at 696-697.

[60] 169 U.S. at 705.

[61] 169 U.S. at 694-705.

[62] 169 U.S. at 675, 682-688.

[63] 169 U.S. at 692.

[64] 169 U.S. at 693.

[65] 169 U.S. at 703; *see also Afroyim v. Rusk*, 387 U.S. 253, 266-267 (1967), which noted at footnote 30 that some have referred to this statement as a holding and others have referred to it as obiter dictum, but which deemed it entitled to great weight regardless of whether it was dictum or a holding.

[66] 169 U.S. at 688.

[67] 112 U.S. 94 (1884).

[68] Anna Williams Shavers, *A Century of Developing Citizenship Law and the Nebraska Influence: A Centennial Essay*, 70 Nebraska L. Rev. 462, 487-489 (1991).

[69] 112 U.S. at 102, 109.

[70] Under *Rogers v. Bellei*, 401 U.S. 815 (1971), the United States Supreme Court's current position appears to be that there are three types of citizenship: the two defined in the

Fourteenth Amendment, birth and naturalization in the United States when subject to the jurisdiction thereof, and non-Fourteenth Amendment statutory citizenship, e.g., the citizenship of Native Americans, persons born abroad to U.S. citizens, and persons born in Puerto Rico, Guam and the Virgin Islands. *See* J. Michael Medina, *The Presidential Qualification Clause in this Bicentennial Year: The Need to Eliminate the Natural Born Citizen Requirement*, 12 Oklahoma City Univ. L. Rev. 253, 265 (1987).

[71] Act of June 2, 1924, c. 233, 43 Stat. 253.

[72] C. 876, §201(b), 54 Stat. 1137, 1158.

[73] C. 477, §301(a)(2), 66 Stat. 163, 235 (1952); codified as amended at 8 U.S.C. §1401(b).

[74] Aliens are seen as willing to enter the United States illegally in order to have a child here, because they realize that when the U.S.-citizen child reaches his/her majority, he/she may bring immediate relatives over to the United States, even if the immigration enforcement authorities decide to deport the parents, or they choose to leave, in the interim. So the automatic birthright gives unauthorized aliens a foot in the door to the United States and its benefits. 157 Cong. Rec. H3096 (daily ed. May 5, 2011) (statement of Rep. King); 151 Cong Rec. E816 (daily ed. April 28, 2005) (statement of Rep. Paul); 149 *Cong. Rec.* E547 (daily ed. March 21, 2003) (statement of Rep. Paul); 143 *Cong. Rec.* H7354-6 (daily ed. September 16, 1997) (statements of Rep. Smith of Texas and Rep. Bilbray); 142 *Cong. Rec.* H2487 (daily ed. March 20, 1996) (statement of Rep. Deal); 141 *Cong. Rec.* E127-8 (daily ed. January 19, 1995) (statement of Rep. Beilenson); 140 *Cong. Rec.* E456 (daily ed. March 16, 1994) (statement of Rep. Taylor); 139 *Cong. Rec.* S11997 (daily ed. September 20, 1993) (statement of Sen. Reid), E 2168-2169 (daily ed. September 15, 1993) (statement of Rep. Gallegly), S10378 (daily ed. August 4, 1993) (statement of Sen. Reid), H4437 (daily ed. July 1, 1993) (statement of Rep. Gallegly), H1005 (daily ed. March 3, 1993) (statement of Rep. Gallegly), E409 (daily ed. February 23, 1993) (statement of Rep. Beilenson); 138 *Cong. Rec.* E2572-3 (daily ed. September 10, 1992) (statement of Rep. Gallegly), E1847 (daily ed. June 16, 1992) (statement of Rep. Gallegly), E441 (daily ed. February 26, 1992) (statement of Rep. Gallegly); 137 *Cong. Rec.* H8180 (daily ed. October 22, 1991) (statement of Rep. Gallegly), H7788 (daily ed. October 10, 1991) (statement of Rep. Dornan).

Senator Inhofe cited the Center for Immigration Studies (CIS), a nonprofit immigration reform organization, and the National Center for Health Statistics for the statistic that in 2002 there were about 383,000 babies born to unauthorized aliens, which represented about 9.5% of all U.S. births in 2002. 152 *Cong. Rec.* S2582 (daily ed. March 30, 2006); see also Steven A. Camarota, CIS, *Backgrounder: Births to Immigrants in America, 1970 to 2002*, at 1, 5, 26, and 28 (July 2005).

Compare these statistics with a more recent statistical analysis done by the Pew Hispanic Center, a Pew Research Center Project, estimating that about 340,000 babies were born to unauthorized aliens in 2008, representing about 8% of all U.S. births in 2008, and that about 4 million U.S.-born children of unauthorized alien parents resided in the United States in 2009. Jeffrey S. Passel and Paul Taylor, Pew Hispanic Center Report, *Unauthorized Immigrants and Their U.S.-Born Children* (August 11, 2010), available at http://pewhispanic.org/reports/report.php?ReportID=125.

[75] The legislative proposals discussed in this report were suggested in Schuck & Smith, *supra* footnote 23, at 116-140, as a more appropriate law of citizenship. Their proposal is to exclude children of unauthorized and nonimmigrant aliens, because the nation has not consented to the permanent residence of the parents. The children of legal residents, i.e., permanent resident aliens, would be provisional citizens at birth and until their majority.

They note that the United Kingdom, which shares common origins with our common law of citizenship, has adopted laws which do not extend birthright citizenship to children of unauthorized or nonimmigrant aliens. For a contrary analysis, see the discussion of different principles/bases for birthright citizenship, including a response to Schuck & Smith and a consideration of the detrimental repercussions of restricting birthright citizenship, in Eisgruber, *supra* footnote 39.

[76] In the 114th Congress, two bills, H.R. 140 and S. 45, have been introduced that would amend INA §301 (8 U.S.C. §1401).

[77] For additional discussion of the detrimental effect of the current birthright citizenship laws, see Wood, *supra* footnote 39, at 493-503. See also *Joint Hearing*, *supra* footnote 39.

[78] For additional criticism of proposals to restrict birthright citizenship and the possible detrimental effect of such legislation, see Margaret Stock, *The Cost to Americans and America of Ending Birthright Citizenship*, National Foundation for American Policy, NFAP Policy Brief, March 2012, http://www.nfap.com/pdf/ NFAPPolicyBrief.Birthright Citizenship.March2012.pdf; Eric Ward, *A New Nativism: Anti-Immigration Politics and the Fourteenth Amendment*, and Margaret D. Stock, *Policy Arguments in Favor of Retaining America's Birthright Citizenship Law*, both in *Made in America: Myths & Facts about Birthright Citizenship*, *supra* footnote 39. See also *Joint Hearing*, *supra* footnote 39.

[79] One should note that the constitutional Citizenship Clause provides the baseline for birthright citizenship—Congress can provide for broader bases by statute. *See supra* footnote 65 and accompanying text.

[80] *E.g.*, H.J.Res. 4, 105th Cong. (1997); H.J.Res. 190, 104th Cong. (1996).

[81] *E.g.*, H.J.Res. 357, 102nd Cong. (1992).

[82] *E.g.*, H.J.Res. 64, 104th Cong. (1995); H.J.Res. 129, 103rd Cong. (1993).

[83] *E.g.*, H.J.Res. 60, 105th Cong. (1997); H.J.Res. 88, 104th Cong. (1995); H.J.Res. 396, 103rd Cong. (1994).

[84] *E.g.*, H.J.Res. 46, 110th Cong. (2007); H.J.Res. 46, 109th Cong. (2005); H.J.Res. 42, 108th Cong. (2003).

[85] *E.g.*, H.J.Res. 56, 104th Cong. (1995); H.J.Res. 117, 103rd Cong., 1st. Sess. (1993).

[86] *E.g.*, H.J.Res. 41, 109th Cong. (2005); H.J.Res. 44, 108th Cong. (2003).

[87] *E.g.*, H.J.Res. 59, 107th Cong. (2001); H.J.Res. 10, 106th Cong. (1999); H.J.Res. 26, 105th Cong. (1997); H.J.Res. 93, 104th Cong. (1995); H.J.Res. 340, 103rd Cong. (1994).

[88] *E.g.*, S.J. Res. 4, 113th Cong. (2013); S.J.Res. 2, 112th Cong. (2011); S.J.Res. 6, 111th Cong. (2009); S.J.Res. 31, 110th Cong. (2008).

[89] *E.g.*, H.R. 3605, 102nd Cong. (1991).

[90] *E.g.*, H.R. 126, 111th Cong. (2009); H.R. 705, 104th Cong. (1995); H.R. 1191, 103rd Cong. (1993).

[91] *E.g.*, H.R. 190, 107th Cong. (2001); H.R. 319, 106th Cong. (1999); H.R. 346, 105th Cong. (1997); H.R. 375, §301, 104th Cong. (1995). These bills specify that the persons in question are either born citizens/nationals of another country of which either of his/her natural parents is a citizen/national or *entitled* upon application to become a citizen/national of that other country.

[92] *E.g.*, H.R. 2162, §701, 104th Cong. (1995); H.R. 4934, §701, 103rd Cong. (1994); H.R. 3862, §401, 103rd Cong. (1994); S. 1351, §1001, 103rd Cong. (1993). These bills specify that the persons in question are either born citizens/nationals of another country of which either of his/her natural parents is a citizen/national or *entitled* upon application to become a citizen/national of that other country.

[93] *E.g.*, H.R. 3938, §701, 109th Cong. (2005); H.R. 4313, §322, 109th Cong. (2005); H.R. 698, 109th Cong. (2005); H.R. 1567, 108th Cong. (2003); H.R. 73, 106th Cong. (1999); H.R. 7, 105th Cong. (1997); H.R. 1363, 104th Cong. (1995). All but the last of these defines "wedlock" as not including common-law marriage.

[94] *E.g.*, H.R. 133, 110th Cong. (2007). The requirements that must be satisfied by the out-of-wedlock father are the same as the requirements that must be satisfied for transmission of citizenship to a child born abroad and out-of-wedlock to a U.S. citizen father under INA §309(a) (8 U.S.C. §1409(a)).

[95] *E.g.*, S. 1269, §503, 110th Cong. (2007); S. 2117, Title V, 109th Cong. (2005).

[96] *E.g.*, H.R. 140, 114th Cong. (2015); S. 45, 114th Cong. (2015); H.R. 140, 113th Cong. (2013); S. 301, 113th Cong. (2013); H.R. 140, 112th Cong. (2011); H.R. 1196, §301, 112th Cong. (2011); S. 723, 112th Cong. (2011); H.R. 994, §301, 111th Cong. (2009); H.R. 1868, 111th Cong. (2009); H.R. 5002, §7, 111th Cong. (2010); H.R. 1940, 110th Cong. (2007); H.R. 6789, §301, 110th Cong. (2008).

[97] International law generally views statelessness as undesirable and seeks to prevent or discourage leaving persons unprotected by and unallied with any nation. The United States apparently is not a party to any conventions or agreements with binding obligations to prevent statelessness. It is unclear whether such an obligation exists under customary international law, although some authorities argue that it does, given the near-universal condemnation of statelessness in the laws of many nations and in various international agreements. *See* 8 Gordon, Mailman & Yale-Loehr, *supra* footnote 12, at §§91.01[3][e] and 100.03[2][e]; J.M Spectar, *To Ban or Not to Ban an American Taliban? Revocation of Citizenship & Statelessness in a Statecentric System*, 39 Cal. W. L. Rev. 263, 296-301 (2003); Christine Biancheria, *Restoring the Right to Have Rights: Statelessness and Alienage Jurisdiction in Light of Abu-zeineh V. Federal Laboratories, Inc.*, 11 Am. U.J. Int'l L. & Pol'y 195, 198-202 (1996); Milton C. Lorenz, Jr., *Note: Aliens— Renunciation of Nationality Leaves Individual Stateless and Excludable as Any Alien*, 46 Tul. L. Rev. 984, 989-990 (1972).

[98] The U.S. Supreme Court has upheld the requirements for transmission of citizenship by a U.S. citizen father to a child born out of wedlock outside the United States as consistent with constitutional equal protection despite the fact that their requirements are more stringent than those for transmission by a U.S. citizen mother to a child born in the same circumstances. *Flores-Villar v. United States*, ___ U.S., 131 S. Ct. 2312; 180 L. Ed. 2d 222 (2011) (affirmed lower appellate court's decision without opinion), and *Nguyen v. Immigration and Naturalization Service*, 533 U.S. 53 (2001). In *Flores-Villar* the Court upheld requirements that the U.S. citizen father must be present in the United States for specific periods of time before the foreign -born child's birth. In *Nguyen* the Court upheld other transmission requirements such as formal legitimation under state law and biological tests establishing paternity that are substantially related to the congressional purpose of requiring a demonstrable bond between the U.S. citizen father and child. In contrast, legislation that eliminates any possibility of basing citizenship on the father's citizenship, nationality, or resident status may be unconstitutional.

[99] H.R. 4192, §201, 110th Cong. (2007); H.R. 3700, §201, 109th Cong. (2005).

[100] H.R. 3534, §213(b), 108th Cong. (2003).

[101] See, for example, Edward J. Erler, *Trump's Critics Are Wrong about the 14th Amendment and Birthright Citizenship*, National Review (Aug. 19, 2015) athttp://www.nati onal revi ew.com/bi rthri ght-citizenshi p-not-mandatedby-constituti on.

[102] 384 U.S. 641, 654-656 (1966).

[103] *See also*, *City of Richmond v. J.A. Croson Co.*, 109 S.Ct. 706, 717-20, 726-727 (1989); *Fullilove v. Klutznick*, 448 U.S. 448, 476-8, 482-4 (1980); *City of Rome v. United States*, 446 U.S. 156 (1980); *Oregon v. Mitchell*, 400 U.S. 112 (1970); THE CONSTITUTION OF THE UNITED STATES OF AM ERICA: ANALYSIS AND INTERPRETATION, S. Doc. No. 112-9, 2209-2210 (Centennial Ed. 2014) (Kenneth R. Thomas, Ed. in Chief, & Larry M. Eig, Managing Ed.) [hereinafter CONSTITUTION ANNOTATED], 2014 pdf file at https://www.congress.gov/constitution-annotated, html version at http://www.crs.gov/conan/details/?mode=topic&doc=Amendment14.xml&t=1|3&s=4#bl2122.

[104] 384 U.S. at 651, n. 10. *See also Mississippi Univ. for Women v. Hogan*, 458 U.S. 718, 731-733 (1982).

[105] CONSTITUTION ANNOTATED, *supra*, footnote 103 at 2210, n. 2131, html at http://www.crs.gov/conan/details/?mode=topic&doc=Amendment14.xml&t=1|3&s=4#bl2131.

[106] *Id.* at 2210-2211, n. 2132, html at http://www.crs.gov/conan/details/?mode=topic&doc=Amendment14.xml&t=1|3&s=4#bl2132.

[107] *Id.* at 2211, html at http://www.crs.gov/conan/details/?mode=topic&doc=Amendment14.xml&t=1|3&s=4#bl2133.

[108] *Fiallo v. Bell*, 430 U.S. 787, 792 (1976); *Mathew v. Diaz*, 426 U.S. 67 (1975); Lem Moon Sing v. United States, 158 U.S. 538, 543 (1895).

[109] *See, e.g.*, *Hernandez-Rivera v. I.N.S.*, 630 F.2d 1352, 1356 (9th Cir. 1980); *Gonzalez-Cuevas v. I.N.S.*, 515 F.2d 1222, 1224 (5th Cir. 1975) *See generally* Annotation, *Infant Citizen as Entitled to Stay of Alien Parents' Deportation Order*, 42 A.L.R. Fed. 924 (1979 & Supp. 2009-10), and Annotation, *What Constitutes "Extreme Hardship" or "Exceptional and Extremely Unusual Hardship," Under §244(a) of Immigration and Nationality Act (8 U.S.C.S. §1254(a)), Allowing Attorney General to Suspend Deportation of Alien and Allow Admission for Permanent Residence*, 72 A.L.R. Fed. 133 §§7-12 (1985 & Supp. 2009-10).

[110] *Urbano de Malaluan v. I.N.S.*, 577 F.2d 589, 594 (9th Cir. 1978). This particular case actually held that suspension of deportation proceedings should be reopened, and it distinguished consideration of the children's existence from a consideration of extreme hardship under proceedings for the suspension of deportation, because the latter proceedings required a seven-year continuous presence in the United States. However, later cases, while acknowledging extreme hardship as a statutory factor, limited review of the immigration court's discretion to grant suspension of deportation and did not seem to consider seven-years continuous presence to be a significant reduction of any loophole based on U.S.-citizen children. *See infra* footnote 111 and footnote 112 and accompanying text. *See also* Annotation, *supra* footnote 109, 72 A.L.R. Fed. at 133, §§7-12. The annotation lists and summarizes a number of cases which do and do not find extreme hardship, including cases involving U.S.-citizen minor children. The specific facts in some cases resulted in a finding of extreme hardship.

[111] *I.N.S. v. Jong Ha Wang*, 450 U.S. 139, 145 (1981).

[112] *I.N.S. v. Rios-Pineda*, 471 U.S. 444, 446, 451 (1985).

[113] 450 U.S. at 145.

[114] Section 201(b)(2)(A)(I) of the Immigration and Nationality Act, codified as amended at 8 U.S.C. §1151(b)(2)(A)(i).

[115] *Hernandez-Rivera v. I.N.S.*, 630 F.2d at 1356, citing *Urbano de Malaluan v. I.N.S.*, 577 F.2d at 594.

[116] *Hernandez-Rivera v. I.N.S.*, 630 F.2d at 1356.

[117] SCHUCK & SMITH, *supra* footnote 23, at 117. For other discussions of case law and legislative history regarding the Fourteenth Amendment, see *Birthright Citizenship Hearing, supra* footnote 39; *Dual Citizenship, Birthright citizenship, and the Meaning of Sovereignty, Hearing Before the Subcommittee on Immigration, Border Security, and Claims of the Committee on the Judiciary, House of Representatives*, Serial No. 109-63, 109th Cong. (2005); *Hearing Before the Subcommittee on Immigration and Claims of the Committee on the Judiciary, House of Representatives, on H.R. 7, Citizenship Reform Act of 1997, and H.R. 1428, Voter Eligibility Verification Act*, Serial No. 23, 105th Cong. (1997).

[118] 169 U.S. at 705.

[119] *United States v. Wong Kim Ark*, 169 U.S. at 693-694. The Court also states:

> The real object of the Fourteenth Amendment of the Constitution, in qualifying the words, "All persons born in the United States," by the addition, "and subject to the jurisdiction thereof," would appear to have been to exclude, by the fewest and fittest words, (besides children of members of the Indian tribes, standing in a peculiar relation to the National Government, unknown to the common law,) [*sic*] the two classes of cases—children born of alien enemies in hostile occupation, and children of diplomatic representatives of a foreign State—both of which, as has already been shown, by the law of England, and by our own law, from the time of the first settlement of the English colonies in America, had been recognized exceptions to the fundamental rule of citizenship by birth within the country. [Citations omitted.]

169 U.S. at 682.

[120] Shavers, *supra* footnote 68, at 489.

[121] *See, e.g., I.N.S. v. Rios-Pineda*, 471 U.S. at 446; *Braun v. I.N.S.*, 992 F.2d 1016, 1020 (9th Cir. 1993); *Hernandez-Rivera v. I.N.S.*, 630 F.2d at 1356; *Wang v. I.N.S.*, 622 F.2d 1341, 1348 (9th Cir. 1980);*Urbano de Malaluan v. I.N.S.*, 577 F.2d at 594; *Gonzalez-Cuevas v. I.N.S.*, 515 F.2d at 1224.

[122] SCHUCK & SMITH, *supra* footnote 23, at 95-98. See also Lino A. Graglia, *Birthright Citizenship for Children of Illegal Aliens: an Irrational Public Policy*, 14 Tex. Rev. Law & Pol. 1 (2009) (arguing that the federal courts should recognize the irrationality of interpreting the Constitution as mandating birthright citizenship for children of unauthorized aliens and permit Congress to legislate birthright citizenship based on public policy discouraging the detrimental effects of expansive birthright citizenship). This article cites Judge Richard Posner's concurring opinion in *Oforji v. Ashcroft*, 354 F.3d 609, 620-21 (7th Cir. 2003), in which he argues:

> ... Congress should rethink ... awarding citizenship to everyone born in the United States (with a few very minor exceptions, ... [citation omitted]), including the children of illegal immigrants whose sole motive in immigrating was to confer U.S. citizenship on their as yet unborn children. This rule, though thought by some compelled by section 1 of the Fourteenth Amendment, which provides that "all persons born or naturalized in the United States, and subject to the jurisdiction thereof, are citizens of the United States and of the State wherein they reside," and in any event codified in 8 U.S.C. §1401(a), which provides that "the following shall be nationals and citizens of the United States at birth: (a) a person born in the United States, and subject to the jurisdiction thereof," makes no sense....
>
> We should not be encouraging foreigners to come to the United States solely to enable them to confer U.S. citizenship on their future children. But the way to stop that abuse of hospitality is to remove the incentive by changing the rule on citizenship,.... A constitutional amendment may be required to change the rule whereby birth in this country automatically confers U.S. citizenship, but I doubt it. [Citation omitted.] The purpose of the rule was to

grant citizenship to the recently freed slaves, and the exception for children of foreign diplomats and heads of state shows that Congress does not read the citizenship clause of the Fourteenth Amendment literally. Congress would not be flouting the Constitution if it amended the Immigration and Nationality Act to put an end to the nonsense.
However, the opinion of the court majority in the *Oforji* case asserts, "The law is clear that citizen family members of illegal aliens have no cognizable interest in preventing an alien's exclusion [citations omitted]. Under the present law a woman who is otherwise a deportable alien does not have any incentive to bear a child (who automatically becomes a citizen) whose rights to stay are separate from the mother's obligation to depart." 354 F.3d at 618.

[123] 59 L. Ed. 2d 578, 124 S. Ct. 2633 (2004). *Amicus Curiae* briefs addressing the interpretation of the Citizenship Clause were submitted by (1) the Eagle Forum Education and Legal Defense Fund; (2) the Claremont Institute Center for Constitutional Jurisprudence; and (3) the Center for American Unity, Friends of Immigration Law Enforcement, National Center on Citizenship and Immigration, and Representatives Steve King, Dana Rohrabacher, Lamar S. Smith, Thomas G. Tancredo, Roscoe Bartlett, Mac Collins, Joe Barton, and John J. Duncan, Jr. Ultimately, Hamdi was released by the United States and allowed to return to Saudi Arabia on the condition that he renounce his U.S. citizenship. Eric Lichtblau, *U.S., Bowing to Court, to Free 'Enemy Combatant,'* N.Y. TIMES (September 23, 2004).

[124] See Maarten P. Vink and Gerard-René de Groot, *Birthright Citizenship. Trends and Regulations in Europe*, at 4 and 20 (November 2010) (noting also a parallel trend of *ius sanguinis* countries broadening citizenship by adopting *ius soli* elements), available at http://eudo-citizenship.eu/docs/birthright_comparativepaper.pdf; Constance A. Johnson, Law Library Of Congress Report 2010-004604, *Birthright Citizenship In G-20 Countries* (August 2010), available at http://www.loc.gov/law/help/reports/pdf/2010-004604_G-20_chart.pdf; U.S. Citizenship and Immigration Services, *Citizenship in the United States*, at 5 and Appendix II at 69 (2004).

In: Birthright Citizenship …
Editor: Garrett Manning

ISBN: 978-1-63485-258-6

Chapter 3

TESTIMONY OF LINO A. GRAGLIA, A.W. WALKER CENTENNIAL CHAIR IN LAW, UNIVERSITY OF TEXAS AT AUSTIN SCHOOL OF LAW. HEARING ON "BIRTHRIGHT CITIZENSHIP: IS IT THE RIGHT POLICY FOR AMERICA?"*

It is difficult to imagine a more irrational and self-defeating legal system than one that makes unauthorized entry to this country a criminal offense and simultaneously provides perhaps the greatest possible inducement to illegal entry a grant of American citizenship. How can such a legal system have come to be and be permitted to continue? The answer, its defenders will tell you, is "the Constitution." Justice Robert Jackson's famous reply to this argument was that the Constitution is not a "suicide pact."

The basis of the constitutional claim of birthright citizenship is the Citizenship Clause of the Fourteenth Amendment, which states: "All persons born or naturalized in the United States, and subject to the jurisdiction thereof, are citizens of the United States and of the State wherein they reside." Not everyone born in the United States is automatically a citizen; only those "subject to the jurisdiction" of the United States.

How should this jurisdiction requirement be interpreted? Like any writing, or at least any law, it should be interpreted to mean what it was intended to

* This is an edited, reformatted and augmented version of testimony presented April 29, 2015 before the House Judiciary Committee, Subcommittee on Immigration and Border Security.

mean by those who adopted it, the ratifiers of the Fourteenth Amendment in 1868. They could not have meant to grant birthright citizenship to children of illegal aliens because, for one thing, there were no illegal aliens in 1868, because there were no restrictions on immigration. The purpose of the Fourteenth Amendment was to constitutionalize the 1866 Civil rights Act which begins with the statement from which the Citizenship Clause of the Fourteenth Amendment is derived: "All persons born in the United States *and not subject to any foreign power* are hereby declared to be citizens of the United States." The phrase "and not subject to any foreign power" seems clearly to exclude children of resident aliens, legal as well as illegal. The Fourteenth Amendment Citizenship Clause substituted the phrase "and subject to the jurisdiction thereof," but there is no indication of an intent to change the original meaning.

Senators Lyman Trumbull of Illinois and Jacob Howard of Ohio, the principal authors of the citizenship clauses in both the 1866 Act and the Fourteenth Amendment, both stated that "[s]ubject to the jurisdiction of the United States" means "[n]ot owing allegiance to anybody else." This would seem clearly to exclude birthright citizenship for the children of legal resident aliens and, *a fortiori,* of illegal aliens. It appears, therefore, that the Constitution, far from requiring the grant of birthright citizenship to children of illegal aliens, is better understood as denying the grant.

The Supreme Court has never ruled directly on the question, but it has spoken to similar issues. In the 1873 *Slaughter-House Cases,* it stated, in dicta, that "the phrase 'subject to the jurisdiction thereof' was intended to exclude from [birthright citizenship] children of ministers, consuls and *citizens or subjects of foreign States,* born within the United States." More important, in 1884 in *Elk v. Wilkins,* the Court held that a child born to members of an Indian tribe did not have birthright citizenship, because although born in the United States, it was not born "subject to the jurisdiction thereof." "[N]o one," the Court said, can become a citizen of a nation without its consent." There cannot be a more total or forceful denial of consent to a person's citizenship than to make that person's presence in the nation illegal.

A possible impediment to this conclusion is the Court's 1898 decision in *United States v Wong Kim Ark,* holding that the Citizenship Clause granted birthright citizenship to children born in the United States of legal resident aliens. Two dissenting justices argued correctly that "the rule making locality of birth the criterion of citizenship" is based on ancient English common law and did not survive the American Revolution. Every European country, including Great Britain has now rejected that rule.

Whatever the merits (or lack of merit) of *Wong Kim Ark* as to the children of legal resident aliens, it does not settle the question of birthright citizenship as to children of *illegal* resident aliens or of children born of legally admitted aliens who have overstayed their visa. Although there is no Supreme Court decision on that question, it has been referred to in some dicta, most importantly in *Plyler v. Doe,* a 1982 five to four decision, in which the Court in a footnote interpreted *Wong Kim Ark* as holding that "no plausible distinction ... can be made between legal and illegal resident aliens." That statement cannot settle the matter, however, because it is not only pure dictum but is based on a mistaken understanding of *Wong Kim Ark.*

The Federal Government's apparent assumption that the children of illegal aliens have birthright citizenship as a constitutional right is, therefore, clearly subject to challenge. A recent scholarly study of the issue concluded that "[t]he framers of the Citizenship Clause had no intention of establishing a universal rule of birthright citizenship," and that Congress has the authority to reject that rule.

Judge Richard Posner agrees: "Congress," he said, "should rethink ... awarding citizenship to everyone born in the United States ... including the children of illegal immigrants whose sole motive in immigrating was to confer U.S. citizenship on their as yet unborn children." "We should not be encouraging foreigners to come to the United States solely to enable them to confer U.S. citizenship on their future children." He concluded, that "Congress would not be flouting the Constitution if it amended the *Immigration and Nationality Act* to put an end to the nonsense."

In my opinion, a law ending birthright citizenship for the children of illegal aliens should and likely would survive constitutional challenge. The Constitution should not be interpreted to require an absurdity.

In: Birthright Citizenship …
Editor: Garrett Manning
ISBN: 978-1-63485-258-6

Chapter 4

TESTIMONY OF DR. JOHN C. EASTMAN, FOUNDING DIRECTOR, THE CLAREMONT INSTITUTE CENTER FOR CONSTITUTIONAL JURISPRUDENCE. HEARING ON "BIRTHRIGHT CITIZENSHIP: IS IT THE RIGHT POLICY FOR AMERICA?"*

Good afternoon, Subcommittee Chairman Gowdy, Ranking Member Lofgren and other Members of the Subcommittee. I am delighted to be with you today as you take up once again what I consider to be an extremely important inquiry with profound consequences for our very notion of citizenship and sovereignty. As a few of the longer- serving members of this Committee may recall, I testified before this Committee back in 2005 at a hearing entitled "Dual Citizenship, Birthright Citizenship, and the Meaning of Sovereignty." The Supreme Court had just recently decided the case of Yaser Esam Hamdi, an enemy combatant who had been captured fighting for the Taliban against U.S. forces in Afghanistan and ultimately transferred to the detention facility at the U.S. Naval Base in Guantanamo Bay, Cuba.[2] When U.S. military officials discovered that Hamdi had been born in Baton Rouge, Louisiana, they began treating him as a U.S. citizen as a result of that birth on U.S. soil even those his parents were both subjects of the Kingdom of Saudi

---

* This is an edited, reformatted and augmented version of testimony presented April 29, 2015 before the House Judiciary Committee, Subcommittee on Immigration and Border Security.

Arabia at the time, residing only temporarily in Louisiana while his father held a temporary visa to work as a chemical engineer on a project for Exxon.[3]

The Supreme Court's holding in the case did not address whether Hamdi was actually a citizen[4]—Justices Scalia and Stevens even referred to him as merely a "presumed citizen"[5]—and the Court has never actually *held* that anyone who happens to make it to U.S. soil can unilaterally bestow U.S. citizenship on their children merely by giving birth here. Although such an understanding of the Fourteenth Amendment has become widespread in recent years, it is not the understanding of those who drafted the Fourteenth Amendment, or of those who ratified it, or of the leading constitutional commentators of the time. Neither was it the understanding of the Supreme Court when the Court first considered the matter in 1872, or when it considered the matter a second time a decade later in 1884, or even when it considered the matter a third time fifteen years after that in the decision many erroneously view as interpreting the Fourteenth Amendment to mandate automatic citizenship for anyone and everyone born on U.S. soil, whether their parents were here permanently or only temporarily, legally or illegally, or might even be here as enemy combatants seeking to commit acts of terrorism against the United States and its citizens.

As I describe more fully below, the modern view ignores—or misunderstands—a key phrase in the Citizenship Clause, which sets out two criteria for automatic citizenship rather than just one. Mere birth on U.S. soil is not enough. A person must be both "born or naturalized in the United States" *and* "subject to its jurisdiction" in order to be granted automatic citizenship. Congress remains free to offer citizenship more broadly than that, of course, pursuant to its plenary power over naturalization granted in Article I, Section 8 of the Constitution, but it has done so. Current law merely parrots the "birth" and "subject to the jurisdiction" requirements that are the floor for automatic citizenship already set by the Constitution.

With the ever-increasing waves of illegal immigration into this country undermining the policy judgments Congress has made about the extent of immigration that should be allowed, it is particularly important to get the birthright citizenship issue right, as the mistaken notion about it has provided a powerful magnet for illegal immigration for far too long. Worse, it has encouraged a trade in human trafficking that has placed at great risk millions of men, women, and children who have succumbed to the false siren's song of birthright citizenship. I am therefore heartened that this Committee is giving serious thought once again to correcting the misinterpretation of this important provision of our Constitution.

I. The Citizenship Clause of the Fourteenth Amendment

To counteract the Supreme Court's decision in *Dred Scott v. Sanford* [6] denying citizenship not just to Dred Scott, a slave, but to all African-Americans, whether slave or free, the Congress proposed and the states ratified the Citizenship Clause of the Fourteenth Amendment, which specifies: "All persons born or naturalized in the United States, and subject to the jurisdiction thereof, are citizens of the United States and of the State wherein they reside."[7] It is today routinely believed that, under the Clause, mere birth on U.S. soil is sufficient to confer U.S. citizenship. Legal commentator Michael Dorf, for example, noted some years back that "Yaser Esam Hamdi was born in Louisiana. Under Section One of the Fourteenth Amendment, he is *therefore* a citizen of the United States, even though he spent most of his life outside this country."[8] What Dorf's formulation omits, of course, is the other component of the Citizenship Clause. One must also be "subject to the jurisdiction" of the United States in order constitutionally to be entitled to citizenship.

To the modern ear, Dorf's formulation nevertheless appears perfectly sensible. Any person entering the territory of the United States—even for a short visit; even illegally—is considered to have subjected himself to the jurisdiction of the United States, which is to say, subjected himself to the laws of the United States. Indeed, former Attorney General William Barr has even contended that one who has never entered the territory of the United States subjects himself to its jurisdiction and laws by taking actions that have an effect in the United States.[9] Surely one who is actually born in the United States is therefore "subject to the jurisdiction" of the Unites States, and entitled to full citizenship as a result.

However strong this interpretation is as a matter of contemporary common parlance, is simply does not comport with either the text or the history surrounding adoption of the Citizenship Clause, or with the political theory underlying the Clause.

Textually, such an interpretation would render the entire "subject to the jurisdiction" clause redundant—anyone who is "born" in the United States is, under this interpretation, necessarily "subject to the jurisdiction" of the United States—and it is a well-established doctrine of legal interpretation that legal texts, including the Constitution, are not to be interpreted to create redundancy unless any other interpretation would lead to absurd results.[10]

A. The 1866 Civil Rights Act, Which the 14th Amendment Was Intended to Codify, Clearly Limits Automatic Citizenship to Those "Not Subject to Any Foreign Power"

Historically, the language of the 1866 Civil Rights Act, from which the Citizenship Clause of the Fourteenth Amendment (like the rest of Section 1 of the Fourteenth Amendment) was derived so as to provide a more certain constitutional foundation for the 1866 Act, strongly suggests that Congress did *not* intend to provide for such a broad and absolute birthright citizenship. The 1866 Act provides: "All persons born in the United States, *and not subject to any foreign power*, excluding Indians not taxed, are hereby declared to be citizens of the United States."[11] As this formulation makes clear, any child born on U.S. soil to parents who were temporary visitors to this country and who, as a result of the foreign citizenship of the child's parents, remained a citizen or subject of the parents' home country, was not entitled to claim the birthright citizenship provided in the 1866 Act.

B. Despite Its Slightly Different Phrasing, the Fourteenth Amendment Codified the Citizenship Language of the 1866 Act

The Fourteenth Amendment was specifically designed to codify the provisions of the 1866 Civil Rights Act and to place that act beyond the ability of a future Congress to repeal. Nevertheless, because the jurisdiction clause of the Fourteenth Amendment is phrased somewhat differently than the jurisdiction clause of the 1866 Act, some have asserted that the difference dramatically broadened the guarantee of automatic citizenship contained in the 1866 Act. The positively-phrased "subject to the jurisdiction" of the United States might easily have been intended to describe a broader grant of citizenship than the negatively-phrased language from the 1866 Act, the argument goes, one more in line with the contemporary understanding accepted unquestioningly by Dorf that birth on U.S. soil is alone sufficient for citizenship. But the relatively sparse debate we have regarding this provision of the Fourteenth Amendment does not support such a reading. When pressed about whether Indians living on reservations would be covered by the clause since they were "most clearly subject to our jurisdiction, both civil and military," for example, Senator Lyman Trumbull, a key figure in the drafting and adoption of the Fourteenth Amendment, responded that "subject to the jurisdiction" of the United States meant subject to its "complete" jurisdiction; "[n]ot owing allegiance to anybody else." And Senator Jacob Howard, who introduced the language of the jurisdiction clause on the floor of the Senate, contended that it should be construed to mean "a full and complete jurisdiction," "the same jurisdiction in extent and quality as applies to every citizen of the United States now" (i.e., under the 1866 Act). That meant that the children of Indians who still "belong[ed] to a tribal relation" and hence owed allegiance to another sovereign (however dependent the sovereign was) would not qualify for citizenship under the clause. The switch from the "not subject to any foreign power" clause of the 1866 Act to the "subject to the jurisdiction" clause of the 14th Amendment simply avoided the concern that the Indian tribes might be deemed within rather than without the grant of automatic citizenship because they were "domestic" rather than "foreign" sovereign powers. Because of this interpretative gloss, provided by the authors of the provision, an amendment offered by Senator James Doolittle of Wisconsin to explicitly exclude "Indians not taxed," as the 1866 Act had done, was rejected as redundant.[12]

There is other evidence in the legislative history as well. During the debate over the 1866 Act, for example, Edgar Cowan, a one-term Senator from Pennsylvania, claimed disparagingly that the bill would "have the effect of naturalizing the children of Chinese and Gypsies born in this country." Senator Trumbull, the bill's lead manager, answered "Undoubtedly." But when Senator Cowan elaborated on the point during debate over the Fourteenth Amendment, it became clear that he was speaking about people who were mere "sojourners" to the United States, here only temporarily and without any obligation of allegiance to the United States, and he would not support an amendment that he mistakenly believed treated as citizens the children born on U.S. soil to such individuals. The response from Senator Conness of California was telling, for he claimed that Senator Cowan's concerns had no relevance "to the first section of the constitutional amendment before us," namely, the Citizenship Clause. Senator Cowan's concerns had no relevance because the Citizenship Clause was not understood by those who drafted it and those who voted for it to cover people only subject to the *territorial* jurisdiction of the United States by virtue of (and only so long as) their temporary presence within the borders of the United States.

Indeed, as Senator Howard repeatedly pointed out, the proposed amendment would "not, of course, include persons born in the United States who are foreigners, aliens, who belong to the families of ambassadors or foreign ministers accredited to the Government of the United States, but will include every other class of persons."[13] It was limited, as Senator Trumbull pointed out several times, to those who were subject to the "complete jurisdiction" of the United States, not merely a temporary and partial jurisdiction. And in response to a concern raised by Senator Johnson that the courts might erroneously interpret the "subject to the jurisdiction clause" to cover Indians because they were subject to our laws—that is, subject to our territorial jurisdiction—Senator Trumbull responded that Indians were not covered ("except in reference to those who are incorporated into the United States as some are, and are taxable and become citizens," as he noted during the 1866 Act debate[14]) because "they are not subject to our jurisdiction in the sense of owing allegiance solely to the United States." In other words, mere presence on U.S. soil was not enough; that subjected one only to the territorial jurisdiction of our laws, but it did not make one subject to the "complete jurisdiction, the allegiance-owing jurisdiction that the drafters of the clause intended. Think of it this way: foreign tourists visiting the United States subject themselves to the laws of the United States while here. An Englishman must drive on the right side of the road rather than the left, for example, when visiting here. But they do not owe allegiance to the United States, they do not get to exercise any part of the political power of the United States, and they cannot be tried for treason if they take up arms against the United States. They are subject only to the partial, territorial jurisdiction while here, but not to the broader jurisdiction that would follow them beyond the borders, the more complete jurisdiction intended by the Fourteenth Amendment.

C. The Ratification Debates Confirm That the Citizenship Clause Did Not Cover Those Who Were Subject to a Foreign Power

Of course, the statements of those who drafted the language of the Fourteenth Amendment and those who voted in Congress to propose it to the States does not necessarily reflect what the amendment's language meant to those who ratified it, and it is the latter who actually give the amendment its binding constitutional authority. But what little evidence we have from the ratification debates in the States confirms rather than detracts from the understanding of the clause discussed above.

Reports about the debates in the Louisiana legislature over ratification of the Fourteenth Amendment that were published in the New Orleans Tribune, for example, confirm the general understanding. On June 18, 1866, for example, the paper reported that the proposed amendment's Citizenship Clause meant the same thing as the language in the 1866 Act: "This [language] is the reiteration of the declaration in the Civil Rights Bill that every person born in the United States and not subject of a foreign power is an American citizen," the paper reported. This followed its earlier report of January 9, 1866, that the amendment which had been proposed provided for equal privileges for all naturalized citizens and "among persons born on its soil of parents permanently resident there."

The same understanding of the language's meaning was expressed over in Alabama, both by those who supported and those who opposed ratification. The Clark County Journal reported on May 10, 1866, for example, that "Section 1 [of the Fourteenth Amendment] reaffirms the Civil Rights Act and incorporates it into the Constitution." On the other side of the ratification fight, the Union Springs Times reported that Section 1 "legitimized" the "bastard" Civil Rights Act.

D. The Supreme Court Adopts the Allegiance Understanding

The interpretative gloss offered by Senators Trumbull and Howard was also accepted by the Supreme Court—by both the majority and the dissenting justices—in *The Slaughter-House Cases*. The majority correctly noted that the "main purpose" of the Clause "was to establish the citizenship of the negro." It added that "[t]he phrase, 'subject to its jurisdiction' was intended to exclude from its operation children of ministers, consuls, *and* citizens or subjects of foreign States born within the United States,"[15] thereby rejecting the claim advanced by some recent scholars, discussed above, that "subject to the jurisdiction" only excluded the children of diplomats. Justice Steven Field, joined by Chief Justice Chase and Justices Swayne and Bradley in dissent from the principal holding of the case, likewise acknowledged that the Clause was designed to remove any doubts about the constitutionality of the 1866 Civil Rights Act, which provided that all persons born in the United States were as a result citizens both of the United States and the state in which they resided, provided they were not at the time subjects of any foreign power.[16]

Although the statement by the majority in *Slaughter-House* was *dicta*, the position regarding the "subject to the jurisdiction" language advanced there was subsequently adopted by the Supreme Court in the 1884 case addressing a claim of Indian citizenship, *Elk v. Wilkins*.[17] The Supreme Court in that case rejected the claim by an Indian who had been born on a reservation and subsequently moved to non-reservation U.S. territory, renouncing his former tribal allegiance. The Court held that the claimant was not "subject to the jurisdiction" of the United States at birth, which required that he be "not merely subject in some respect or degree to the jurisdiction of the United States, but completely subject to their political jurisdiction, and owing them direct and immediate allegiance."[18] John Elk did not meet the jurisdictional test because, as a member of an Indian tribe at his birth, he "owed immediate allegiance to" his tribe and not to the United States. Although "Indian tribes, being within the territorial limits of the United States, were not, strictly speaking, foreign states," "they were alien nations, distinct political communities," according to the Court.[19] Drawing explicitly on the language of the 1866 Civil Rights Act, the Court continued:

> Indians born within the territorial limits of the United States, members of, and owing immediate allegiance to, one of the Indian tribes, (an alien though dependent power,) although in a geographical sense born in the United States, are no more "born in the United States and subject to the jurisdiction thereof," within the meaning of the first section of the fourteenth amendment, than the children of subjects of any foreign government born within the domain of that government, or the children born within the United States, of ambassadors or other public ministers of foreign nations.[20]

Indeed, if anything, Indians, as members of tribes that were themselves dependent to the United States (and hence themselves subject to its jurisdiction), had a stronger claim to citizenship under the Fourteenth Amendment merely by virtue of their birth within the territorial jurisdiction of the United States than did children of foreign nationals. But the Court in *Elk* rejected that claim, and in the process necessarily rejected the claim that the phrase, "subject to the jurisdiction" of the United States, meant merely territorial jurisdiction as opposed to complete, political jurisdiction.

Such was the interpretation of the Citizenship Clause initially given by the Supreme Court. As Thomas Cooley noted in his treatise, The General Principles of Constitutional Law in America, "subject to the jurisdiction" of the United States "meant full and complete jurisdiction to which citizens are generally subject, and not any qualified and partial jurisdiction, such as may consist with allegiance to some other government."

II. The Supreme Court's *Holding* in the 1898 *Wong Kim Ark* Case Is Limited to Lawful, Permanent Residents; Its Broader *Dicta* Is Erroneous and Has Never Been Adopted by the Court

The Supreme Court next confronted the Citizenship Clause in 1898, in the case of *United States v. Wong Kim Ark.*[21] Here, I must confess that the actual holding of the case (as opposed to its dicta) is a much closer call than I believed when I testified before this Committee back in 2005. Wong Kim Ark was a citizen, the Court held, because he was "born in the United States, of parents of Chinese descent, who at the time of his birth were subjects of the emperor of China, but have a permanent domicile and residence in the United States." I had previously focused on the Court's description of Wong Kim Ark's parents as being "subjects of the emperor of China," which should, standing alone, have placed Wong Kim Ark outside the scope of the automatic citizenship guaranteed by the Fourteenth Amendment because he would have been, through them, "subject to the jurisdiction" of another power. But I have come to appreciate that the issue was more complicated than that. Not only were Wong Kim Ark's parents lawful, permanent residents in the United States, but they were also "domiciled" in the United States, a legal term of art that conveys more than mere temporary residence but a fixed and permanent home. Moreover, they had not taken more formal steps to demonstrate allegiance to the United States (by becoming citizens, for example, and renouncing their former allegiance) because a U.S. treaty with the emperor of China foreclosed that possibility. In other words, Wong Kim Ark's parents had become as subject to the complete jurisdiction of the United States (and not just the territorial jurisdiction) as we had allowed. Under those circumstances, it is not a surprise that the Supreme Court held that Wong Kim Ark was a citizen because he had been born on U.S. soil to parents who were lawfully and permanently "domiciled" here. But that is the limit of the actual holding in the case.

To be sure, Justice Horace Gray, writing for the Court, spoke more broadly, and it is that *obiter dictum* that has erroneously come to be viewed in recent years as having established that birth on U.S. soil alone is sufficient for automatic citizenship, no matter the circumstances. After correctly noted that the language to the contrary in *The Slaughter-House Cases* was merely dicta and therefore not binding precedent,[22] Justice Gray made several errors in his own *dicta.* He found the *Slaughter-House* dicta unpersuasive, for example, because of a subsequent decision holding that foreign consuls (unlike ambassadors) were "subject to the jurisdiction, civil and criminal, of the courts of the country in which they reside,"[23] thereby demonstrating confusion about the critical distinction between partial, territorial jurisdiction, which subjects all who are present within the territory of a sovereign to the jurisdiction of its laws, and complete, political jurisdiction, which requires as well allegiance to the sovereign.

More troubling than his rejection of the persuasive *dicta* from *Slaugher-House* was the fact that Justice Gray also repudiated the actual holding in *Elk v. Wilkins*, which he himself had authored. After quoting extensively from the opinion, including the portion, reprinted above, noting that the children of Indians owing allegiance to an Indian tribe were no more "subject to the jurisdiction" of the United States within the meaning of the Fourteenth Amendment than were the children of ambassadors and other public ministers of foreign nations born in the United States, Justice Gray simply claimed, without any analysis, that *Elk* "concerned only members of the Indian tribes within the United States, and had no tendency to deny citizenship to children born in the United States of foreign parents of Caucasian, African, or Mongolian descent, not in the diplomatic service of a foreign country."[24]

By limiting the "subject to the jurisdiction" clause to the children of diplomats, who neither owed allegiance to the United States nor were (at least at the ambassadorial level) subject to its laws merely by virtue of their residence in the United States as the result of the long-established international law fiction of extraterritoriality by which the sovereignty of a diplomat is said to follow him wherever he goes, Justice Gray simply failed to appreciate what he seemed to have understood in *Elk*, namely, that there is a difference between territorial jurisdiction and the more complete, allegiance-obliging jurisdiction that the Fourteenth Amendment codified.

Justice Gray's failure even to address, much less appreciate, the distinction between territorial jurisdiction and complete, political jurisdiction was taken to task by Justice Fuller, joined by Justice Harlan, in dissent. Drawing on an impressive array of legal scholars, from Vattel to Blackstone, Justice Fuller correctly noted that there was a distinction between two sorts of allegiance—"the one, natural and perpetual; the other, local and temporary." The Citizenship Clause of the Fourteenth Amendment referred only to the former, he contended. He contended that the absolute birthright citizenship urged by Justice Gray was really a lingering vestige of a feudalism that the

Americans had rejected, implicitly at the time of the Revolution, and explicitly with the 1866 Civil Rights Act and the Fourteenth Amendment.

Quite apart from the fact that Justice Fuller's dissent was logically compelled by the text and history of the Citizenship Clause, Justice Gray's broad interpretation led him to make some astoundingly incorrect assertions. He claimed, for example, that "a stranger born, for so long as he continues within the dominions of a foreign government, owes obedience to the laws of that government, *and may be punished for treason*."[25] That is simply not true, as allegiance to the sovereign is a necessary prerequisite for a charge of treason.[26] Justice Gray also had to recognize dual citizenship as a necessary implication of his position,[27] despite the fact that, ever since the Naturalization Act of 1795, "applicants for naturalization were required to take, not simply an oath to support the constitution of the United States, but of absolute renunciation and abjuration of all allegiance and fidelity to every foreign prince or state, and particularly to the prince or state of which they were before the citizens or subjects."[28] That requirement still exists though it no longer seems to be taken seriously. Hopefully this Committee will, as a result of these hearings, begin to address that fundamental contradiction in our naturalization practice.

Finally, Justice Gray's broader *dicta* is simply at odds with the notion of consent that underlay the sovereign's power over naturalization. What it meant, fundamentally, was that foreign nationals could secure American citizenship for their children unilaterally, merely by giving birth on American soil, whether or not their arrival on America's shores was legal or illegal, temporary or permanent, with the consent of the United States or explicitly contrary to its consent.

Justice Gray believed that the children of only two classes of foreigners were not "subject to the jurisdiction" of the United States and therefore not entitled to the birthright citizenship he thought guaranteed by the Fourteenth Amendment. First, as noted above, were the children of ambassadors and other foreign diplomats who, as the result of the fiction of extraterritoriality, were not even considered subject to the territorial jurisdiction of the United States. Second were the children of invading armies born on U.S. soil while it was occupied by the foreign army. But apart from that, all children of foreign nationals who managed to be born on U.S. soil were, in his formulation, citizens of the United States. Children born of parents who had been offered permanent residence but were not yet citizens and who as a result had not yet renounced their allegiance to their prior sovereign would become citizens by birth on U.S. soil. This was true even if, as was the case in *Wong Kim Ark* itself, the parents were, by treaty, unable ever to become citizens.

Children of parents residing only temporarily in the United States on a work or student visa, such as Yaser Hamdi's parents, would also become U.S. citizens. Children of parents who had overstayed their temporary visa would also become U.S. citizens, even though born of parents who were now here illegally. And, perhaps most troubling from the "consent" rationale, children of parents who never were in the United States legally would also become citizens as the direct result of the illegal action by their parents. This would be true even if the parents were nationals of a regime at war with the United States and even if the parents were here to commit acts of sabotage against the United States, at least as long as the sabotage did not actually involve occupying a portion of the territory of the United States. The notion that the framers of the Fourteenth Amendment, when seeking to guarantee the right of citizenship to the former slaves, also sought to guarantee citizenship to the children of enemies of the United States who were in our territory illegally, is simply too absurd to be a credible interpretation of the Citizenship Clause.

III. Reviving Congress's Constitutional Power Over Naturalization

This is not to say that Congress could not, pursuant to its naturalization power, choose to grant citizenship to the children of foreign nationals. But thus far it has not done so. Instead, the language of the current naturalization statute simply tracks the minimum constitutional guarantee—anyone born in the United States, *and subject to its jurisdiction*, is a citizen. With the absurdity of Hamdi's claim of citizenship so recently and vividly before us, it is time for the courts, and for the political branches as well, to revisit Justice Gray's erroneous *dicta* purporting to interpret that language, and to restore to the constitutional mandate what its drafters actually intended, that only a complete jurisdiction, of the kind that brings with it a total and exclusive allegiance, is sufficient to qualify for the automatic grant of citizenship to which the people of the United States actually consented when they adopted the Fourteenth Amendment.

Of course, Congress has in analogous contexts been hesitant to exercise its own constitutional authority to interpret the Constitution in ways contrary to the pronouncements of the Courts. Even if that course is warranted in most situations so as to avoid a constitutional conflict with a co-equal branch of the government, it is not warranted here for at least two reasons. First, as the Supreme Court itself has repeatedly acknowledged, Congress's power over naturalization is "plenary," while "judicial power over immigration and naturalization is extremely limited."[29] While that recognition of plenary power does not permit Congress to dip below the constitutional floor, of course, it does counsel against any judicial interpretation that provides a broader grant of citizenship than is actually supported by the Constitution's text, history, and theory.

Second, the gloss that has been placed on the *Wong Kim Ark* decision is actually much broader than the actual holding of the case. This Committee should therefore recommend, and Congress should then adopt, a narrow reading of the decision that does not intrude on the plenary power of Congress in this area any more than the actual holding of the case requires. Wong Kim Ark's parents were actually in this country both legally and permanently, yet were barred from ever pursuing citizenship (and renouncing their former allegiance) by a treaty that closed that door to all Chinese immigrants. They were therefore as fully subject to the jurisdiction of the United States as they were legally permitted to be, and under those circumstances, it is at least arguable that the Citizenship Clause extends birthright citizenship to their children. But the effort to read *Wong Kim Ark* more broadly than that, as interpreting the Citizenship Clause to confer birthright citizenship on the children of those *not* subject to the full and sovereign (as opposed to territorial) jurisdiction of the United States, not only ignores the text, history, and theory of the Citizenship Clause, but it permits the Court to intrude upon a plenary power assigned to Congress itself. Yaser Hamdi's case has highlighted for us all the dangers of recognizing unilateral claims of birthright citizenship by the children of people only temporarily visiting this country, and highlighted even more the dangers of recognizing such claims by the children of those who have arrived illegally to do us harm. It is time for Congress to reassert its plenary authority here, and make clear, by resolution, its view that the "subject to the jurisdiction" phrase of the Citizenship Clause has meaning of fundamental importance to the naturalization policy of the nation.

Because the promise of citizenship has become one of the three most significant magnets for illegal immigration to this country—which is to say, one of the three things that most seriously undermines Congress's considered policy judgments about the level of immigration that can be sustained, it is extremely important that we get back to the correct understanding of what the Constitution actually requires, and especially what it does not require.

I understand that a bill has been introduced in the House that would do just that. It confirms that children born on U.S. soil to parents, at least one of whom is a U.S. "citizen or national," are "subject to the jurisdiction" as contemplated by the Fourteenth Amendment and therefore automatic citizens at birth. It recognizes the actual holding of *Wong Kim Ark* and deems children born on U.S. soil to "an alien admitted for permanent residence in the United States whose residence is in the United States" are likewise "subject to the jurisdiction" for purposes of the Fourteenth Amendment. And the bill adds an important additional category of children who are properly deemed automatic citizens at birth under this allegiance-owing understanding of the "subject to the jurisdiction" requirement, namely, the children of those serving in the armed forces of the United States who, by virtue of their service, have already taken an oath of allegiance to the United States.

As important as clarifying what the Fourteenth Amendment covers is clarifying what it does not cover, however. The bill currently does that only implicitly, in a provision that states the bill should not be construed to affect the citizenship or nationality status of anyone born before the effective date of the Act. With a slight addition, this provision can make explicit what is now only implicit, namely, that this retroactive grant of citizenship to people who were not "subject to the jurisdiction" of the United States at the time of their birth in the way that phrase is properly understood, is made pursuant to Congress's plenary power over naturalization, not because of some perceived mandate of the Fourteenth Amendment.

I applaud this Committee's efforts in beginning the process to address this problem, and I look forward to working with you and the Committee's staff to help in your efforts to clarify an important constitutional requirement, the misinterpretation of which is beginning to have profound implications for the very idea of sovereignty.

End Notes

[1] Henry Salvatori Professor of Law & Community Service and former Dean, Chapman University Dale E. Fowler School of Law; Ph.D., M.A., The Claremont Graduate School; JD., The University of Chicago Law School; B.A., The University of Dallas. The views expressed herein are those of Dr. Eastman and not necessarily those of the Universities with which he is or has been affiliated. Dr. Eastman is also a Senior Fellow at the Claremont Institute and the Founding Director of its Center for Constitutional Jurisprudence, in which capacity he appeared as *amicus curiae* before the Supreme Court in *Hamdi v. Rumsfeld*, 542 U.S. 507

(2004), addressing the issue of birthright citizenship. He previously testified before this Subcommittee on the subject in September 2005.

[2] Brief of the United States, *Hamdi v. Rumsfeld*, at 6-7.

[3] *See* Certificate of Live Birth, Birth No. 117-1980-058-00393, on file in the Vital Records Registry of the State of Louisiana and available at http://news.findlaw.com/cnn/docs/terrorism/hamdi92680birthc.pdf (last visited March 20, 2003); Frances Stead Sellers, *A Citizen on Paper Has No Weight*, Wash. Post B1 (Jan. 19, 2003).

[4] Rather, in an opinion by Justice O'Connor, the Court held that Hamdi had a right to challenge the factual basis for his classification and detention as an enemy combatant. *Hamdi v. Rumsfeld*, 542 U.S. 507, 124 S.Ct. 2633, 2635 (2004). As the Supreme Court later made clear, that right did not turn on whether or not Hamdi was a citizen, for the Due Process clause applies not just to citizens but to all "persons." *See Boumediene v. Bush*, 553 U.S. 723 (2008) (holding that other combatants who were clearly not citizens could bring a habeas petition because that provision, like the Due Process Clause of the Fifth Amendment, applied to all "persons" and not just citizens).

[5] *Hamdi v. Rumsfeld*, 542 U.S. 507, 124 S.Ct. 2633, 2660 (2004) (Scalia, J., dissenting).

[6] 60 U.S. 393 (1857).

[7] U.S. Const. Amend. XIV, § 1.

[8] Michael C. Dorf, *Who Decides Whether Yaser Hamdi, Or Any Other Citizen, Is An Enemy Combatant?* FindLaw (Aug. 21, 2002) (emphasis added).

[9] *See, e.g.*, The Legality as a Matter of Domestic Law of Extraterritorial Law Enforcement Activities that Depart from International law: Hearings before the Subcomm. on Civil and Constitutional Rights of the House Comm. on the Judiciary, 101st Cong., 1st Sess. 3 (1989) (statement of William Barr, U.S. Assistant Attorney General); William J. Tuttle, *The Return of Timberlane? The Fifth Circuit Signals a Return to Restrictive Notions of Extraterritorial Antitrust*, 36 Vanderbilt J. Transnat'l L. 319, 348 (Jan. 2003) (noting that in April 1992 then-Attorney General William Barr revised Department of Justice antitrust enforcement guidelines to permit lawsuits against foreign corporations who acted exclusively outside the United States if their operations were detrimental to U.S. exporters); *see also United States v. Noriega*, 117 F.3d 1206 (11th Cir. 1997).

[10] *See, e.g.*, Posner, *Legal Formalism, Legal Realism, and the Interpretation of Statutes and the Constitution*, 37 Case. W. Res. L. Rev. 179 (1989); *Gustafson v. Alloyd Co., Inc.*, 513 U.S. 561, 562 (1995) ("this Court will avoid a reading which renders some words altogether redundant"). Some have argued that the "subject to the jurisdiction" clause serves to exclude foreign diplomats from the reach of the citizenship clause, and is therefore not entirely redundant with the "birth" clause. Quite apart from the fact that there is not a shred of evidence in the legislative or ratification history to support such a purpose, the explanation does not work. Because of the diplomatic fiction of "extraterritoriality" that an ambassador is the sovereign presence of his home nation even while in the United States, the ambassador's children are not "born . . . in the United States," and the "subject to the jurisdiction" clause, therefore, does not provide any additional limtiation.

[11] Chapter 31, 14 Stat. 27 (April 9, 1866).

[12] Congressional Globe, 39th Cong., 1st Sess., 2892-97 (May 30, 1866). For a more thorough discussion of the debate, see Peter H. Schuck and Rogers M. Smith, Citizenship Without Consent: Illegal Aliens in the American Polity 72-89 (Yale Univ. Press 1985).

[13] Cong. Globe, at 2890 (May 30, 1866). Particularly noteworthy is the fact that, in this discussion, Senator Howard said that the Citizenship Clause would exclude not just the families of ambassadors but others who are "foreigners, aliens" as well—in other words,

anyone who retained their allegiance to a foreign sovereign. That distinction, though perhaps not perfectly clear from the passage quoted above, becomes undeniable when considered in light of Senator Howard's very next comment, in response to a proposed amendment to exclude "Indians not taxed." "Indians born within the limits of the United States, and who maintain their tribal relations, are not, in the sense of this amendment, born "subject to the jurisdiction of the United States," he said. Instead, [t]hey are regarded, and always have been in our legislation and jurisprudence, as being *quasi* foreign nations." *Id.*

[14] Cong. Globe, at 498 (Jan. 30, 1866).

[15] 83 U.S. (16 Wall.) 36, 73 (1872).

[16] *Id.* at 92-93.

[17] 112 U.S. 94 (1884).

[18] *Id.* at 102.

[19] *Id.* at 99.

[20] *Id.* at 102.

[21] 169 U.S. 649 (1898).

[22] 169 U.S. at 678.

[23] *Id.* at 679 (citing, e.g., 1 Kent, Comm. 44; *In re Baiz*, 135 U.S. 403, 424 (1890)).

[24] *Id.* at 681-82.

[25] *Id.* at 693.

See 18 U.S.C.A. § 2381 ("Whoever, *owing allegiance to the United States*, levies war against them or adheres to their enemies, giving them aid and comfort within the United States or elsewhere, is guilty of treason") (emphasis added).

[27] *Id.* at 691.

[28] *Id.* at 711 (Fuller, J., dissenting) (citing Act of Jan. 29, 1795, 1 Stat. 414, c. 20)

[29] *See, e.g., Miller v. Albright*, 523 U.S. 420, 455 (1998); *Fiallo v. Bell*, 430 U.S. 787, 792 (1977); *Kleindienst v. Mandel*, 408 U.S. 753, 769-770 (1972); *Galvan v. Press*, 347 U.S. 522, 531 (1954).

In: Birthright Citizenship …
Editor: Garrett Manning

ISBN: 978-1-63485-258-6

Chapter 5

STATEMENT OF JON FEERE, LEGAL POLICY ANALYST, CENTER FOR IMMIGRATION STUDIES. HEARING ON "BIRTHRIGHT CITIZENSHIP: IS IT THE RIGHT POLICY FOR AMERICA?"*

Thank you, Chairman Gowdy, Ranking Member Lofgren and distinguished Members of the Subcommittee for the opportunity to testify on the issue of birthright citizenship.

Every year, 350,000 to 400,000 children are born to illegal immigrants in the United States. To put this another way, as many as one out of 10 births in the United States is now to an illegal immigrant mother. Despite the foreign citizenship and illegal status of the parent, the Executive Branch automatically recognizes these children as U.S. citizens upon birth, providing them Social Security numbers and U.S. passports. The same is true of children born to tourists and other aliens who are present in the United States in a legal but temporary status. It is unlikely that Congress intended such a broad application of the 14th Amendment's Citizenship Clause, and the Supreme Court has only held that children born to citizens or permanently domiciled immigrants must be considered U.S. citizens at birth. Some clarity from Congress would be helpful in resolving this ongoing debate.

---

* This is an edited, reformatted and augmented version of a statement presented April 29, 2015 before the House Judiciary Committee, Subcommittee on Immigration and Border Security.

While it is unclear for how long the U.S. government has followed this practice of universal, automatic "birthright citizenship" without regard to the duration or legality of the mother's presence, the issue has garnered increased attention for a number of reasons.

First, the mass illegal immigration this country has experienced in recent decades has raised the question of whether Congress intended that the 14th Amendment's Citizenship Clause would operate to turn children of illegal aliens into U.S. citizens at birth. The population of U.S.-born children with illegal alien parents has expanded rapidly in recent years from 2.7 million in 2003 to 4.5 million by 2010.[1] Under the immigration enforcement priorities of the Obama administration, illegal immigrants who give birth to U.S. citizens have become low priorities for deportation; furthermore, under the president's DAPA program (the Deferred Action for Parents of Americans and Lawful Permanent Residents program) — a program currently held up in court — would provide benefits to illegal immigrants who gave birth here and allow them to "stay in the U.S. without fear of deportation."[2] The broad interpretation of the Citizenship Clause forms the basis for these policies.

Second is the issue of chain migration. A child born to illegal aliens in the United States can initiate a chain of immigration when he reaches the age of 18 and can sponsor an overseas spouse and unmarried children of his own. When he turns 21, he can also sponsor his parents and any brothers and sisters. Family-sponsored immigration accounts for most of the nation's growth in immigration levels; approximately 2/3 of our immigration flow is family-based. This number continues to rise every year because of the ever-expanding migration chains that operate independently of any economic downturns or labor needs. Although automatic and universal birthright citizenship is not the only contributor to chain migration, ending it would prevent some of this explosive growth.

Third, the relatively modern phenomenon of affordable international travel and tourism has increased the opportunity for non-citizens to give birth here, raising questions about the appropriate scope of the Citizenship Clause. According to the Department of Homeland Security, in 2013 there were 173 million nonimmigrant admissions to the United States. This includes people entering for tourism, business travel, and other reasons, but also those entering to engage in "birth tourism", a growing phenomenon that has arisen in direct response to our government's broad application of the Citizenship Clause. Birth tourism is the practice of people around the world traveling to the United States to give birth for the specific purpose of adding a U.S. passport holder to their family, while misrepresenting the true intention of their visit to the United States.

Birth tourism is becoming much more common with every passing year and Congress will have to address it. Part of that discussion will include a focus on birthright citizenship and whether children born to people in the country on a temporary basis should be considered U.S. citizens. An entire "birth tourism" industry has been created and the phenomenon has grown largely without any debate in Congress or the consent of the public. While many birth tourists currently making news are from China, it certainly is not limited to that country. Birth tourists come from all corners of the globe, from China to Turkey to Nigeria. The Nigerian media reported a few years back that the phenomenon of Nigerians traveling to the United States to give birth is "spreading so fast that it is close to becoming an obsession." The article was in response to congressional legislation aimed at ending birth tourism; the article's title: "American Agitations Threaten a Nigerian Practice."

Birth tourism is also no longer just for the wealthy. The *Los Angeles Times* reports that 'the practice has become particularly popular in recent years with the newly wealthy Chinese middle class." Similarly, a Chinese news article associated with Time Magazine noted that "Giving birth to a child abroad is not a privilege reserved to the stars and the very wealthy. An increasing number of expectant middle-class parents also fancy giving their children passports that they can feel proud of."[5]

Though the number is very difficult to calculate, we estimate that the number of birth tourists coming to the United States each year is very roughly around 35,000 to 36,000 people based on the limited governmental data available.[6] If Congress does not address this, there is every reason to believe the number will grow.

Fourth is the issue of taxpayer-subsidized benefits. Most benefits Americans would regard as "welfare" are not accessible to illegal immigrants. However, illegal immigrants can obtain welfare benefits such as Medicaid and food stamps on behalf of their U.S.-born children. Many of the welfare costs associated with illegal immigration, therefore, are due to the Executive Branch's current interpretation of the Citizenship Clause. Put another way, greater efforts at barring illegal aliens from welfare programs will not significantly reduce costs because their citizen children can continue to access the benefits.

Currently, 71 percent of illegal-alien headed households with children make use of at least one major welfare program. Of illegal-alien headed households with children where the household head is from Mexico, 79 percent make use of at least one major welfare program. By comparison, of households with children headed by a native-born American citizen, 38.7 percent make use of at least one major welfare program.[7]

For these reasons and others, there has been a bipartisan effort to end birthright citizenship legislatively. Multiple legislative efforts to clarify the appropriate scope of the Citizenship Clause have been proposed by both Republican and Democrat politicians, as there remains much debate about who should be considered "subject to the jurisdiction" of the United States. In 1993, Sen. Harry Reid (D-Nev.) introduced legislation what would limit birthright citizenship to the children of U.S. citizens and legally resident aliens, and similar bills have been introduced by other legislators in nearly every Congress since.

FEW COUNTRIES GRANT AUTOMATIC CITIZENSHIP TO CHILDREN OF ILLEGAL IMMIGRANTS

Only 30 of the world's 194 countries grant automatic citizenship to children born to illegal aliens.[9]

Of advanced economies, as rated by the International Monetary Fund, Canada and the United States are the only countries that grant automatic citizenship to children born to illegal aliens.

No European country grants automatic citizenship to children of illegal aliens.

The global trend is moving away from automatic birthright citizenship as many countries that once had such policies have ended them in recent decades. Countries that have ended universal birthright citizenship include the United Kingdom, which ended the practice in 1983, Australia (1986), India (1987), Malta (1989), Ireland, which ended the practice through a national referendum in 2004, New Zealand (2006), and the Dominican Republic, which ended the practice in January 2010.

The reasons countries have ended automatic birthright citizenship are diverse, but have resulted from concerns not all that different from the concerns of many in the United States. Increased illegal immigration is the main motivating factor in most countries. Birth tourism was one of the reasons Ireland ended automatic birthright citizenship in 2004.[9] If the United States were to stop granting automatic citizenship to children of illegal immigrants, it would be following an international trend.

Some countries which currently recognize automatic birthright citizenship are considering changing the policy. For example, Barbados is struggling with large amounts of immigration (relative to its size), both legal and illegal, and is contemplating ending birthright citizenship for children of illegal aliens. The country initiated an illegal alien amnesty in 2009 which gave illegal aliens six months to legalize their status. Anyone still in the country illegally after December 1, 2009, faces deportation. The amnesty had a number of conditions, and any illegal alien with three or more dependents could not automatically qualify. Consequently, the question of what to do with children born to illegal aliens became central to political debate. A series of changes have been recommended by the nation's immigration department, and one proposed change is the end of birthright citizenship.

Not too far from Barbados, a similar discussion has been taking place. Antigua and Barbuda, one of the few nations that currently grant automatic birthright citizenship to children of illegal aliens, in 2010 outlined a series of enforcement-minded recommendations aimed at tightening their citizenship, immigration, and work permit policies. In a government report, the authors note that "the so called 'open door' policy relative to immigration should be discontinued as there is a significant risk of Antigua and Barbuda nationals being displaced in the job market by 'non-nationals' whose willingness to work hard for low wages makes them attractive to prospective employers." The authors also note that work visa issuance should "have as priority the 'importing' of skills needed in Antigua and Barbuda for the growth of the economy." Although the report does not call for a change to birthright citizenship policies, it does note that the "citizenship of Antigua and Barbuda should be treated as a thing of value and worth." Interestingly, when asked about Antigua and Barbuda ending birthright citizenship for illegal aliens, a consular officer with whom I spoke while investigating the issue stated, "probably they might look at it down the road."[1]

There are varying approaches to citizenship throughout the world. Many countries require at least one parent to be a citizen of the country in order for their child to acquire the country's citizenship. Some countries make a distinction between whether that citizen parent is the mother or father. There are other variations as well. In Australia, a country that does not recognize automatic birthright citizenship, a child born to illegal immigrant parents may obtain Australian citizenship at age 10 if he was born after 1986 and has lived in Australia for the entire 10 years.[11] An

Australian official explained to me that the child must still petition the immigration minister, who conducts fact-finding to verify the claim. The official also added that it would be "extremely unlikely" that illegal aliens would be able to remain in Australia for the necessary ten-year period, meaning that the grant of citizenship rarely happens."[2]

It is important to remember that while a country may officially recognize birthright citizenship, it does not mean that the country is necessarily easy on illegal immigration. Paraguay, for example, has a birthright citizenship policy, but it has serious laws against illegal immigration which not only bar the employment of illegal aliens, but also prohibit owners of hotels and guesthouses from providing illegal aliens with accommodations.[13]

Mexico has a unique citizenship policy in that the country's constitution grants automatic nationality to anyone born in Mexico, but not automatic citizenship. This is true even of children born to Mexican citizens. When a Mexican reaches the age of 18, they then acquire citizenship. Mexican government officials with whom I spoke were uncertain how often their country grants nationality or citizenship to children born to illegal immigrants. The effort Mexico makes to discourage immigration indicates that this may be a rare occurrence. For example, the Mexican Constitution, among other things, allows the government to expel any immigrant for any reason without due process.[14] The constitution also severely limits the property rights of immigrants and requires immigrants to get permission from the government to own land; even if permission is granted, the immigrant can never own land within 100 kilometers of land borders nor land within 50 kilometers of the coasts.[15] An immigrant wishing to change these rules will have difficulty as the Mexican Constitution states that only citizens are entitled to participate in Mexico's political affairs.[16] Even with Mexico's form of birthright citizenship, any child born to illegal immigrants or even legal immigrants in Mexico is barred from becoming president of Mexico; not only must the Mexican president be born in Mexico, but so must at least one of his parents." While Mexico may grant citizenship to children born to illegal aliens, the nation's constitution clearly imputes a second-class status on children of immigrants.

Additionally, many countries which do recognize birthright citizenship are not necessarily quick to grant citizenship to all people within their jurisdiction. Some countries are the focus of human rights groups because they do not grant citizenship to indigenous people. For example, Peru, a country with a birthright citizenship policy, has an indigenous population that makes up approximately 45 percent of the nation's total population, but the indigenous do not have access to Peruvian citizenship. Unlike the United States, some countries' birthright citizenship policies come with exceptions.

It is also important to remember that some of the countries which do automatically grant citizenship to children of illegal immigrants may not have much illegal immigration at all. For this reason, comparing countries like Fiji to the United States, for example, may be somewhat disingenuous; Fiji has an estimated illegal immigrant population of 2,000 people, while the United States has an estimated illegal immigrant population of up to 12 million.[18]

Moreover, not all countries which recognize birthright citizenship allow the child to initiate chain migration by petitioning to have additional family members enter. Consequently, some countries are able to avoid some of the problems associated with birthright citizenship experienced in the United States.

Perhaps most instructive is the clarity with which most other nations have authored their respective citizenship laws. Most countries' citizenship laws contain very little ambiguity and do not require one to conduct a historical analysis or seek judicial clarification for the purpose of determining intent. For example, Brazil's constitution confers citizenship on "those born in the Federative Republic of Brazil, even if of foreign parents," Australia's statutory law declares a person born in Australia an automatic Australian citizen "if and only if a parent of the person is an Australian citizen, or a permanent resident, at the time the person is born," while the Dominican Republic's new constitution denies birthright citizenship to "foreigners who are in transit or who reside illegally in Dominican territory."[19]

To the extent there remains any debate over birthright citizenship, it would be helpful for Congress to clarify the scope of the Citizenship Clause of the 14th Amendment.

A CONSTITUTIONAL AMENDMENT IS NOT NECESSARY TO CHANGE THE SCOPE OF THE CITIZENSHIP CLAUSE

A constitutional amendment would likely be necessary if the 14th Amendment's Citizenship Clause clearly directed citizenship be granted to children of temporary aliens. However, there is no evidence that Congress intended that children of tourists or illegal aliens, for example, be included within the scope of the Citizenship Clause.

Some argue that Congress cannot pass legislation relating to matters addressed in the Constitution in an attempt to change the scope or interpretation of amendments. Of course, Congress routinely considers legislation relating to constitutional amendments and a clear example would be any number of pieces of legislation aimed at the 2nd Amendment designed to clarify the appropriate scope of gun rights.[20]

When it comes to the 14th Amendment's Citizenship Clause, there are volumes of writings on the meaning of "subject to the jurisdiction thereof", which would seem to open up the door to some legislative clarification. Furthermore, in the case of the Citizenship Clause, the Congress that authored the amendment had never contemplated the phenomenon of illegal immigration or birth tourism, making it hard to conclude that the Citizenship Clause was designed to include the children of such individuals.

Influential U.S. Court of Appeals Judge Richard Posner has spoken on this topic and included his thoughts on the matter in a case in 2003. He feels that a constitutional amendment would not necessarily be needed to end the practice in the United States and that legislation would be sufficient. He explained: "A constitutional amendment may be required to change the rule whereby birth in this country automatically confers U.S. citizenship, but I doubt it."[21]

Posner concluded: "Congress would not be flouting the Constitution if it amended the Immigration and Nationality Act to put an end to the nonsense." He reasoned that the policy is one that " Congress should rethink" and that the United States "should not be encouraging foreigners to come to the United States solely to enable them to confer U.S. citizenship on their future children."[22]

In fact, there has been a bipartisan effort to end birthright citizenship legislatively. Multiple legislative efforts to clarify the appropriate scope of the Citizenship Clause have been proposed by both Republican and Democrat politicians, as there remains much debate about who should be considered "subject to the jurisdiction" of the United States. In 1993, Sen. Harry Reid (D-Nev.) introduced legislation what would limit birthright citizenship to the children of U.S. citizens and legally resident aliens, and similar bills have been introduced by other legislators in nearly every Congress since.

It may be the case that even legislation is not necessary to change birthright citizenship policy. It is arguable that the Executive Branch could change the way in which the 14th Amendment is applied, particularly in light of President Obama's recent unilateral actions on immigration. The current situation of children born to birth tourists and illegal aliens receiving citizenship has happened due to some past administration allowing agencies to treat these children like the children of U.S. citizens; federal agencies under the watch of the president have granted these children Social Security numbers and U.S. passports for many years. It is unclear whether this has happened by design or whether the agencies simply never gave the issue any consideration. But since Congress has never given any explicit direction on the issue of birthright citizenship as it relates to children of aliens temporarily in the country, it might be reasonable for a president who wants to narrow application of the Citizenship Clause to direct Executive Branch agencies to not consider such children U.S. citizens at birth. Though a president could argue that interpretation and application of the Constitution is part of the president's responsibilities, it is possible that such action would result in litigation which, in turn, would likely result in the Supreme Court weighing in on the matter.

I authored a detailed analysis of the history of birthright citizenship in the United States in a Center for Immigration Studies report titled, "Birthright Citizenship in the United States: A Global Comparison."[23]

Birth Tourists, the Obama Administration's Policies, and Fraud

Birth tourists interpret the 14th Amendment as a means to obtain residency for anyone who travels to the United States on any type of visa. Obviously, our visa systems were not designed to operate in this manner, but there are two things to consider.

First, it has become the case under the Obama administration's immigration enforcement priorities that a person in the country illegally who has a U.S. citizen child is not a top priority for deportation, unless they commit some sort of violent crime. In an administrative and very real sense, giving birth on U.S. soil does allow non-citizens to ignore the parameters of their original visa. They can overstay and have a high level of confidence that they will not be deported.

Second, because of existing immigration law explained earlier, the birth tourist can become a permanent resident of the United States by having their U.S.-born child fill out a petition for them when the child turns 21. Oftentimes the parents will not return to the United States until they are planning on retirement. In a legal sense, engaging in fraud and becoming a birth tourist has become a means to obtaining U.S. citizenship. It is difficult to imagine that the Congress which authored the 14th Amendment and the States which ratified it intended this outcome.

What irks Americans about this situation is that birth tourists are effectively taking control Over U.S. immigration and citizenship policy by turning a grant of *temporary admission into a permanent* stay. The practice of granting automatic birthright citizenship allows a seemingly temporary admission of one foreign visitor to result in a permanent increase in immigration and grants of citizenship that were not necessarily contemplated or welcomed by the American public.

The growth of the birth tourism industry illustrates how the executive branch's broad application of the Citizenship Clause can have the effect of transferring control over the nation's immigration policy from the American people to foreigners.

And there is broad agreement within the immigration debate that birth tourism does constitute fraud. My organization—which supports better enforcement and lower levels of immigration—considers birth tourism to be an act of fraud, as does the Center for American Progress, a group that generally holds positions on immigration that differ from ours.[24] "It's not necessarily illegal to come here to have the baby, but if you lie about your reasons for coming here, that's visa fraud," said Claude Arnold, special agent in charge of Homeland Security Investigations for Los Angeles.[25]

While it is fraud for a person to travel here as a tourist and conceal their real purpose, namely to add a U.S. passport holder to their family, it is unclear whether the federal government has prosecuted such a crime in the case of birth tourism. In the recent case in California, there's no evidence that the government is prosecuting the actual *birth tourists* for fraud. Instead, prosecution seems to be aimed entirely at those operating birth tourism centers.

The statutes that the U.S. could use to go after birth tourists include, but are not limited to:

Fraud and False Statements (18 U.S.C. § 1001). It is common for birth tourists to make false statements to immigration officials during investigations, and to misrepresent themselves and their travel intentions to the government, generally. Any false statement or fraudulent act may be prosecuted under 18 U.S.C. § 1001 as a felony. The falsification does not have to be made directly to a government official; it must simply relate to and affect a relationship "within the jurisdiction" of the federal government.[26] It is broad in scope, and as the courts have noted, §1001 is "intended to serve the vital public purpose of protecting governmental functions from frustration and distortion through deceptive practices, and it must not be construed as if its object were narrow and technical."[27] A person faces a fine and up to five years imprisonment for knowingly and willfully violating this statute.

Fraud and Misuse of Visas, Permits, and Other Documents (18 U.S.C. § 1546). Illegal immigrants often use fraudulent documentation as a means to enter the United States, procure a job, or to obtain certain benefits. As such, this law is frequently used in immigration prosecutions. It may have applicability in birth tourism prosecutions as well since it contains a perjury provision that it applies to anyone who uses a false statement with respect to a material fact in any application or other document required under immigration laws. For example, it has been invoked where an alien has provided false information on an entry form.[28] A basic violation of this law can result in a 10-year jail sentence and/or fine, provided it does not involve terrorism or a drug trafficking.

Conspiracy to Commit Offense or to Defraud the United States (18. U.S.C. § 371). Oftentimes a birth tourist will work with others in order to enter the United States and commit fraud. In such an instance, each party might be violating a conspiracy offense related to defrauding the United States. Specifically, if two or more individuals "conspire either to commit any offense against the United States, or to defraud the United States, or any agency thereof" and one or more of the individuals makes even one small act in furtherance of the conspiracy, each can be fined and/or imprisoned up to five years.[29] This statute has been invoked where illegal aliens have conspired to falsify entry documents,[39] and in the context of illegal aliens transporting and harboring illegal aliens,[31] for example. The government can charge the alien with both conspiracy and the underlying, substantive offense.

Birth Tourism Fraud Results in Additional Fraud. It is often the case that those engaging in illegal activity covered by one area of immigration law also commit other violations of law. In the case of the recent enforcement efforts at birth tourism centers in California, the government found evidence of tax evasion, false tax returns, and willful failure to report foreign bank and financial accounts. The government found that the organizers earned hundreds of thousands of dollars in unreported income from the immigration fraud scheme. According to the affidavit, one organizer received more than

$500,000 in wire transfers and his partner received more than $1.5 million from bank accounts in China."

But the actual birth tourists also are alleged to have defrauded hospitals and taxpayers. In one case, a birth tourist paid just $4,080 of a $28,845 hospital bill, taking advantage of health care meant for the indigent. Investigations revealed that their bank account had charges at Louis Vuitton, Rolex, and the Wynn Las Vegas hotel-casino."

The *Wall Street Journal* explained how some birth tourism operators advertised their services:

> "The website touts the advantages of having a U.S.-born child, including free K-12 education, low tuition and low-interest loans 'to save over 1 million Yuan in four years in college over a foreign student,' government jobs reserved for U.S. citizens, legal immigration to the U.S. for family members who can later enjoy retirement benefits, and less pollution, among many others."[34]

These benefits is why one organizer of birth tourism told one of Time Magazine's partner news agencies that "The return on investment is higher than robbing a bank."[35] The article also detailed the methodologies that birth tourists use to sneak into the United States:

> "When Liu Li boarded a plane for the United States, she had a little bit of makeup on, was wearing a loose dress, and had her hair up. She tried to hold her handbag in front of her belly in a natural way, just as the middleman had taught her. She was trying to look as calm as any wealthy Chinese lady would look when travelling abroad. But Liu Li couldn't help feeling terribly nervous: she was six months pregnant when she left for the United States, where she wanted to give birth to an American citizen.
>
> "Liu Li knew that going through customs would be a lot easier than obtaining a U.S. visa. In order to obtain the tourist visa that enabled her to go to America for the delivery, she had to carefully choose her clothes, and spend a lot of time practicing her walking and interview techniques. She memorized a host of details about her hotel booking and about famous sight-seeing spots so as to convince the Embassy officer that she was just another Chinese woman going shopping in the States."[36]

In other words, the birth tourist was deceiving U.S. officials and engaging in fraud. These techniques are often taught to intending birth tourists by the organizers of the practice. In the recent enforcement effort in California, for example, Chinese birth tourists were told to travel through Hawaii before arriving in Los Angeles so as to give the appearance of tourism travel.

The government's affidavit explains more detail of the recent enforcement effort and is available online.[37] It also notes that several of the birth tourists discovered in the recent effort are employed by the Chinese government.

THE QUESTION OF ASSIMILATION AND WHETHER CHILDREN OF BIRTH TOURISTS CONSIDER THEMSELVES AMERICAN

It is very important for people we allow in on a permanent basis who obtain citizenship to think of themselves as Americans. It is equally important for Americans to think of them as Americans. Assimilating new U.S. citizens is a critical part of our immigration system as it helps maintain the social fabric of America. But a broad interpretation of our nation's birthright citizenship clause is creating situations that threaten to break down the nation's social cohesion.

Meet Jennifer Shih, a UC Davis college student born in New York who tells the *Sacramento Bee*, "*I'm* Taiwanese more than American."[38] Back in 1989, Shih's mother boarded a jet bound for New York, tourist visa in hand. She didn't arrange her travel in order to take in Broadway show, however; she was eight months pregnant and the goal was to add a U.S.-passport holder to her family. In other words, she was engaging in fraud as admitted by Mr. Shih, who cited the quality of American schools as the impetus. Two months after giving birth Mrs. Shih "returned to Taiwan with her U.S. passport-bearing daughter in tow".

In 2004, when Jennifer reached the age of 15, she returned to the United States to take advantage of U.S.-taxpayer subsidized high schools in Idaho, Utah, and college in California. Understandably, Jennifer — who didn't speak English when she arrived — describes the United States as a "foreign country". The reporter who interviewed her notes that "even after eight years', Jennifer says she still "thinks about Taiwan every day" and visits nearly every year. Jennifer's honesty highlights the absurdity of a lax birthright citizenship policy and raises significant questions of allegiance and assimilation.

Jennifer's father has since moved to the United States, presumably as a result of chain migration, which allows individuals to sponsor parents and siblings upon turning 21 years of age. Jennifer says she is interested in having kids of her own who will go to college in America. This is a perfect example of how one instance of fraud from a temporary alien can result in a permanency that was never welcomed by the American public. Birth tourism effectively puts U.S. citizenship policy into the hands of foreigners.

Despite the fact that no one in Jennifer's family has been paying taxes to support the University of California system, she will be treated like every other California student whose parents have been subsidizing the system for decades. As a result of her mother's fraud, Jennifer will pay a tuition rate that is much less than she otherwise would have as a foreign student. And every social welfare program available to Americans will also be available to Jennifer and her father.

Congress should consider whether birth tourists gaming our tourist system in this manner harms the concept of citizenship.

THERE ARE POSSIBLY 36,000 BIRTH TOURISTS PER YEAR

It is difficult to estimate the total number of birth tourists who arrive in the United States each year. There are a few different ways one might come to an estimate, however.[39]

One potential source of data on birth tourism is birth certificate records. The data contained on the forms is based on self-reporting of parents while at the hospital shortly after the baby is born. The data includes their place of birth and their address. No agency verifies the mother's place of birth, address, or any other information on the birth certificate form.

The Centers for Disease Control and Prevention (CDC) reports that 896,363 women who gave birth in 2012 indicated that they were born outside of the United States. If only 2 or 3 percent of these births were to women who are engaging in birth tourism, it would mean the United States sees 18,000 to 27,000 births annually. While this number would be less than 1 percent of the roughly four million annual births in the United States, the aggregate number of birth tourists babies would still be large, especially the cumulative effect over a number of years.

One source of information often cited in the birth tourism debate is likely less helpful than it first appears: the address mothers provide when giving birth. This is the address where mothers want the birth certificate mailed.

In 2012, the government reports that 7,955 women gave an overseas address when filling out their birth certificate paperwork. This number is not helpful for a couple of reasons.

First, it is not at all clear that those engaging in birth tourism provide an overseas address. It is important to remember that those engaging in birth tourism typically stay in the United States with friends, family, or in some other residential setting arranged by those "selling" birth tourism services immediately before and after they have their babies. There is some anecdotal evidence that birth tourist mothers provide the address they stay at before or after giving birth, rather than an address in the mother's home country. The reason for this is that mothers generally seek a U.S. passport for the child and they need the birth certificate to obtain one. This seems to be a common occurrence. In March 2015, CNN reported that one birth tourist used an address in "a high-end Irvine, Calif., apartment complex where one birth tourism company had rented a number of homes" for her newborn's passport application.[40] A *USA Today* report on the investigation notes that the birth tourists were "promised Social Security numbers and U.S. passports for their babies before flying back home."[41] On page 76 of the warrant used in the recent enforcement effort, the government lists "California birth certificates" as one of the items to be seized.[42] While there is evidence that birth tourists provide local addresses to obtain birth certificates, we simply do not know what share of birth tourist mothers provide a U.S. address instead of their overseas address.

Second, some share of those providing an overseas address for the mailing of the birth certificate are U.S. citizens living abroad who returned home to have their child on U.S. soil. These are people who obviously would not be considered birth tourists.

Another way to possibly estimate the prevalence of birth tourism is to compare administrative data and Census Bureau data. The American Community Survey (ACS), collected annually by the Bureau asks women if they had a child in the prior 12 months. The survey is designed to reflect the U.S. population as of July 1 of the year the survey was taken, so the survey is recording the number of women living in the country at mid-year who had a child in the last half of the prior year and the first half of the year of the survey.

The public-use file of the 2012 ACS shows that there were 863,407 foreign-born women who indicated that they had a child in the prior 12 months.

In the second half of 2011 and the first half of 2012, the CDC reports 898,975 births to foreign-born mothers.

The difference between these two numbers is 35,568 and implies that about 36,000 foreign-born women gave birth in the United States in the 12 months before July 1, 2012, but were no longer in the country. While there are a number of important caveats about this number, this comparison provides some idea of the possible number of babies born to birth tourist mothers.

Some of the caveats to consider include: (1) it is unknown what share of births are not recorded in state birth records compiled by the CDC; (2) there is both a margin of error in the ACS and some undercount of foreign-born women in that data; (3) some foreign-born women may have had a child and left the country, but they did so after many years of residence and perhaps would not be considered birth tourists; (4) a person who comes as a birth tourist but has a miscarriage is not included in the birth records as only live births are included in the state birth data collected by the CDC. However, such a person should still be considered a birth tourist.

Birthright Citizenship for Children of Foreign Diplomats?

Amid the debate over the proper scope of the 14th Amendment's Citizenship Clause, there is one area of solid agreement among advocates on all sides: In the least, children born to foreign diplomats are not "subject to the jurisdiction" of the United States and are therefore not to be granted U.S. citizenship.

But a lack of direction from Congress has resulted in children born to foreign diplomats on U.S. soil receiving U.S. birth certificates and Social Security numbers (SSNs) — effectively becoming U.S. citizens in the eyes of some government agencies — despite the limiting language within the Citizenship Clause of the 14th Amendment.

It may be the case that the limiting language in the Citizenship Clause has nearly no practical effect. This issue was the focus of two of my reports, "Birthright Citizenship for Children of Foreign Diplomats?" and "Why the Citizenship Clause Should Be Taken More Seriously."[43]

There is no federal requirement that hospitals ask new parents if they are foreign diplomatic staff. State agencies do not instruct hospitals to differentiate between children born to diplomatic staff and those born to U.S.

citizens or temporary or illegal aliens. Hospitals issue the same birth certificates to all newborns.

The Social Security Administration (SSA) does not investigate whether SSN requests are for children of foreign diplomats. Although the agency does recognize that U.S.-born children of foreign diplomats are not eligible to receive SSNs, and although they admit it should not be happening, there is no mechanism in place for preventing such issuance.

In order to end the practice of granting automatic U.S. citizenship to children of foreign diplomats, Congress could author regulations requiring declaration of parental diplomatic status on birth certificate request forms. As an alternative, Congress could require parents to have SSNs before a U.S. birth certificate or SSN is issued to a newborn. While this latter proposal might create better results and be more easily administered, it would have the effect of ending automatic birthright citizenship not just for children of diplomats, but also for children of illegal aliens and temporary aliens — an outcome that is arguably more aligned with the intended scope of the 14th Amendment than the outcome created by current practices.

The birth certificate and SSN are so critical to verifying identification in the United States that it behooves Congress to direct federal agencies to be a little more careful in issuing documents that, when combined, create the appearance of U.S. citizenship. If children born to foreign diplomats are, as the State Department told me, "entitled" to U.S. birth certificates, then Congress should consider requiring use of different birth certificates for those not born "subject to the jurisdiction" of the United States. Better regulation of SSN issuance is also necessary.

The State Department appears to have some difficulty keeping track of children born on U.S. soil to foreign diplomats. I have spoken with a number of attorneys and other officials at the State Department (in a number of offices), and they explained that they do not keep track of children born to foreign diplomats. An official at the Office of Foreign Missions (OFM), which some researchers have argued keeps track of children born to foreign diplomats, explained that his office has not been tasked with maintaining a database of children born to foreign diplomats. The official explained that there are data sets that may contain the names of children born to foreign diplomats on U.S. soil, but that it would be completely dependent on the parent alerting the State Department's Office of Protocol to the fact that the diplomat had a child. The OFM official explained, "We all share the same data system, but we [the OFM] don't input that data and we don't directly have authority over that issue."

Officials at the Office of Protocol, which seemed to have the most information on the subject (and an office to which I was directed a number of times while researching the matter), explained that a list of children born to foreign diplomats would be "impossible to compile." I pressed again, asking whether there was any kind of list maintained by that office. The official's response:

> “No, no, no. We don't keep a list. What we do is register any employee working at an embassy or consulate... But when it comes to dependents, like in this case when the children are born here, we send a memo to the Office of American Citizen Services, they follow up with our case, they are the ones who make the determinations.”

I asked, “I guess it also depends whether or not the foreign diplomat even alerts you to them having a child, right?”

The official's response: “Exactly.”

I spoke with Office of American Citizen Services, which directed me to a section of their department called the Office of Overseas Citizenship. That office was surprised that the inquiry had been directed to them and felt that it was the Protocol Office that might be compiling a list of children born to foreign diplomats: “I believe, my strong suspicion is that that is the Office of Protocol. If someone from the Office of Protocol told you that, that would be interesting.” And later: “I have to say it would be Protocol making that list. It would not be us. I'm quite sure. If someone told you to come to us, and if I'm telling you to go to them, I wonder if there is such a list, and I'm dubious.”

Multiple officials in this office shared the same sentiment. From my research, it does not seem that any government agency is keeping track of children born to foreign diplomats. The question, then, is whether the limiting language in the 14th Amendment's Citizenship Clause has any practical effect.

A key issue is that some government agencies consider U.S. birth certificates and SSNs to indicate U.S. citizenship, despite the fact that children of foreign diplomats are receiving them. According to the U.S Citizenship and Immigration Services, a “birth certificate provides proof of citizenship.”

I spoke with the Office of Personnel Management (OPM) which oversees employment for government jobs requiring U.S. citizenship. In an e-mail, the agency explained, “OPM does not utilize the Department of State for verification of U.S. citizenship for persons born in the United States.” The problem, of course, is that some people born in the United

States are not to be considered U.S. citizens — children born to foreign diplomats (if not others), and the State Department seems to be the only agency that might begin to have the capacity to keep track. Since children born to foreign diplomats have U.S. birth certificates and validly-issued SSNs, they do not raise any red flags for the OPM, even though they certainly should. If the children were issued birth certificates that read, "Not Evidence of U.S. Citizenship" and if they were not automatically granted SSNs, they would not be able to acquire a job reserved for U.S. citizens as easily as they may be able to do so today.

Since the U.S. is granting documents that give the appearance of U.S. citizenship to anyone and everyone at birth, the only option for OPM (and underlying agencies seeking employees) at this point would be to run the names of all job applicants through the State Department before clearing a person as an authorized U.S. citizen. Of course, this would be a significant undertaking, and it would depend on the State Department having a complete list of all children born to foreign diplomats — something that does not appear to be happening. Multiple officials at the State Department explained that they have never heard of the OPM coming to their agency for vetting purposes. Stopping such careless issuance of documents at the outset might be the best way to make sure non-citizens are not acquiring jobs that require U.S. citizenship.

There are more problems with this lack of focus on the birthright citizenship issue as it relates to children of foreign diplomats and they are detailed in the reported mentioned earlier, but one more point is worth noting: USCIS considers children born to foreign diplomats to be Legal Permanent Residents (LPR) at birth, though that was not always the case (8 § C.F.R. 1101.3). A couple of unpublished, decades-old court decisions made this so, and it is a questionable grant, not just because it raises plenary power issues (i.e. the right of the political branches to set immigration policy), but also because it seems to go against the intent of the 14th Amendment. Prior to these decisions, the government considered these children non-immigrants. As LPRs, these children become eligible for naturalization after five years.

The State Department is currently rewriting the agency's guidelines on birthright citizenship, signaling a possibly significant departure from current 14th Amendment jurisprudence. In 1995, the State Department's "Foreign Affairs Manual" (FAM) straightforwardly declared that children born on U.S. soil to foreign diplomats are not to be considered U.S. citizens:

> "Under international law, diplomatic agents are immune from the criminal jurisdiction of the receiving state. Diplomatic agents are also immune, with limited exception, from the civil and administrative jurisdiction of the state. The immunities of diplomatic agents extend to the members of their family forming part of their household. For this reason children born in the United States to diplomats to the United States are not subject to U.S. jurisdiction and do not acquire U.S. citizenship under the 14th Amendment or the laws derived from it."[44]

While the reasoning attempts to push the idea that being "subject to the jurisdiction thereof" means the same thing as being susceptible to police force, such an interpretation is implausible.[45]

Nevertheless, the conclusion is correct and no serious scholar or immigration advocacy organization has argued that children born to foreign diplomats should be granted citizenship.

Despite the clarity of this guideline, the Obama administration has been developing new rules on the issue of children born to foreign diplomats. The most recent FAM has eliminated the language above and replaced it with a promise of new guidelines:

> "Children of Foreign Diplomats: 7 FAM 1100 Appendix J (under development) provides extensive guidance on the issue of children born in the United States to parents serving as foreign diplomats, consuls, or administrative and technical staff accredited to the United States, the United Nations, and specific international organizations, and whether such children are born 'subject to the jurisdiction of the United States.'"[46]

An inquiry into the status of Appendix J made mid-2011 revealed that the State Department was expecting to publish the changes by the end of 2011. However, it appears as if the Appendix was never created or at least never made available to the public.

End Notes

[1] Jeffrey S. Passel and D'Vera Cohn, "A Portrait of Unauthorized Immigrants in the United States," Pew Hispanic Center, Apr. 14, 2009, www.pewhispanic.orafilesireports/107.pdf. "A Nation of Immigrants A Portrait of the 40 Million, Including 11 Million Unauthorized," Jan. 29, 2013. http://www.pewhispanic.org/2013/01/29/a-nation-of-immigrants/ Note: These figures do not include children who are 18 years of age or older nor those who are married, meaning the actual figure is somewhat larger.

[2] 'Executive Actions on Immigration', U.S. Citizenship and Immigration Services. http://www.uscis.gov/immigrationaction.

[3] Katie Foreman and Randall Monger, 'Nonimmigrant Admissions to the United States: 2013', Dep't of Homeland Security, Office of Immigration Statistics, July 2014. http://www.dhs.gov/sites/defaultifiles/publications/ois ni fr 2013.pdf .

[4] Victoria Kim and Frank Shyong, "Maternity tourism' raids target California operations catering to Chinese," Los Angeles Times, Mar. 3, 2015. http://www.latimes.com/local/lanow/la-me-In-birth-tourism-schemes-raids20150303- story.html#page=1.

[5] Jon Feere, 'Birth Tourism Fraud from China: 'The return on investment is higher than robbing a bank'," Center for Immigration Studies, June 16, 2011. http://cis.org/feere/birth-tourism-fraud-from-china.

[6] Steven Camarota, 'There Are Possibly 36,000 Birth Tourists Annually', Center for Immigration Studies. April 2015. http://www.cis.org/camarota/there-are-possibly-36000-birth-tourists-annually.

[7] Steven Camarota, 'Welfare Use by Immigrant Households with Children," Center for Immigration Studies, Apr. 2011. http://cis.org/immigrant-welfare-use-2011.

[8] Jon Feere, 'Birthright Citizenship in the United States: A Global Comparison," Center for Immigration Studies, Aug 2010. http://cis.org/birthright-citizenship.

[9] See, e.g., 'Citizenship tourists," The Economist, Jun. 3, 2004. http://www.economist.com/node/2734580.

[10] Ms. E. Ann Henry et al., Report on Review of Matters Pertaining to Immigration, Work Permits, Citizenship and Electoral Reform, Gov't of Antigua and Barbuda, Feb. 9, 2010, www.ab.gov.ag/gov v3/pdf/immigration report.pdf.

[11] Automatic acquisition of citizenship on 10th birthday 'A child born in Australia on or after 20 August 1986, who did not acquire Australian citizenship at birth, automatically acquires it on their 10th birthday if they have been ordinarily resident in Australia for 10 years from birth. This provision operates regardless of the parent/s immigration or citizenship status," www.immi.gov.au/media/fact-sheets/17nz.htm.

[12] Conversation with Rose Lacey, Citizenship and Migration Officer, Australian High Commission, May 31, 2010.

[13] Para. Const. art. 69.

[14] Mex. Const. tit. I, ch. III, art. 33, http://info.juridicas.unam.mx/infjur/leg/constmex/pdf/consting.pdf.

[15] Mex. Const. tit. I, ch. I, art. 27.

[16] Mex. Const. tit. I, ch. I, art. 9.

[17] Mex. Const. tit. III, ch. III, art. 82.

[18] Kalinga Seneviratne, 'Islanders welcome Chinese cash, but not Chinese," Asia Times Online, Sept. 17, 2002, http://www.atimes.comiatimes/China/D117Ad04.html.

[19] Braz. Cont. tit. II, ch. III, art. 12, http://www.v-brazil.com/government/laws/titlell.html; Australian Citizenship Act 2007, pt. II, div. 1. (2007), http://www.comlaw.gov.au; Dom. Rep. Const. ch. V, § 1, art. 18, http://www.imarcano.com/mipais/politicos/title1.html.

[20] Pete Kasperowicz, 'Ten gun bills on Congress's first day,' The Hill, Jan. 3, 2013. http://thehill.com/blogs/flooraction/house/275587-10-gun-bills-introduced-in-first-day-of-the-house (citing a number of pieces of legislation, including Rep. Sheila Jackson Lee's (D-Texas) proposed H.R. 65, which would raise the eligibility age to carry a handgun from 18 to 21.).

[21] Oforji v. Ashcroft, 354 F.3d 609, 620-1 (2003).

[22] Id.

[23] Jon Feere, 'Birthright Citizenship in the United States: A Global Comparison,' Center for Immigration Studies, Aug. 2010. http://www.cis.org/birthright-citizenship

[24] CNN Debate, 'The Maternity Tourism Business,' Apr. 19, 2011. http://cis.org/ Videos/KrikorianDebatesBirthrightCNN.

[25] Andrew Blankstein, Anna R. Schecter and Tracy Connor, 'Feds Raid California 'Maternity Hotels' for Birth Tourists,' NBC News, Mar. 3, 2015. http://www.nbcnews.com/news/us-news/feds-raid-california-maternityhotels-birth-touristsn315996

[26] See United States v. Munoz, 392 F. Supp. 183 (E.D. Mich. 1974).

[27] Ogden v. United States, 303 F.2d 724, 742 (9th Cir. 1962). See also United States v. Rodgers, 466 U.S. 475 (1984) (upholding a broad interpretation of the scope of § 1001); see also Brogan v. United States, 522 U.S. 398 (1998).

[28] See, e.g., United States v. Wiggan, 673 F.2d 145 (6th Cir. 1982).

[29] 18 U.S.C. § 371 (2013). Note: If the offense toward which the conspiracy is aimed is a only a misdemeanor, the punishment for such conspiracy will not exceed the maximum punishment provided for such misdemeanor.

[30] See, e.g., Shimi Miho v. United States, 57 F.2d 491 (9th Cir. 1932).

[31] See, e.g., Matter of Roman, Interim Decision #3095, A-37431891, December 16, 1988.

[32] Miriam Jordan, 'Federal Agents Raid Alleged 'Maternity Tourism' Businesses Catering to Chinese,' Wall Street Journal, Mar. 3, 2015. http://www.wsi.com/articles/us-agents-raid-alleged-maternity-tourism-anchorbabybusinesses-catering-to-chinese-1425404456.

[33] Michael Winter, 'Feds raid Chinese 'birth tourism' rings in California,' USA Today, Mar. 3, 2015. http://www.usatoday,com/story/news/2015/03/03/california-chinese-birth-tourism-raids/24338087/

[34] Miriam Jordan, 'Federal Agents Raid Alleged 'Maternity Tourism' Businesses Catering to Chinese,' Wall Street Journal, Mar. 3, 2015. http://www.wsi.corn/articles/us-agents-raid-alleged,maternity-tourism-anchorbabybusinesses-catering-to-chinese-1425404456.

[35] Jon Feere, 'Birth Tourism Fraud from China: The return on investment is higher than robbing a bank',' Center for Immigration Studies, June 16, 2011. http://cis.org/feere/birth-tourism-fraud-from-china.

[36] Id.

[37] http://i2.cdn.turner.com/cnn/2015/images/03/03/birth.tourism.pdf.

[38] Jon Feere, "Birth Tourism Baby Calls United States a "Foreign Country", Center for Immigration Studies, Sept. 28, 2012. http://cis.orefeere/birth-tourism-baby-calls-united-states-foreign-country.

[39] Steven Camarota, "There Are Possibly 36,000 Birth Tourists Annually", Center for Immigration Studies, Apr. 2015. http://www.cis.orkticamarota/there-are-possibly-36000-birth-tourists-annually.

[40] Sophia Yan, "How far Chinese moms will go to have U.S. babies," CNN, Mar. 30, 2015. http://money.cnn.com/2015/03/30/news/china-moms-birth-tourism-fraud/

[41] Michael Winter, "Feds raid Chinese 'birth tourism' rings in California," USA Today, Mar. 3, 2015. http://www.usatoday.com/story/news/2015/03/03/california-chinese-birth-tourism-raids/24338087/

[42] http://12.cdn.turner.cornicnn/2015/images/03/03/birth.tourism.pdf.

[43] Jon Feere, "Birthright Citizenship for Children of Foreign Diplomats? Limiting Language in the 14th Amendment's Citizenship Clause Has No Practical Effect," Center for Immigration Studies, July 2011. http://cis.orabirthrightcitizenship-diplomats & Jon Feere, "Why the Citizenship Clause Should Be Taken More Seriously: A Response to Margaret Stock",

Center for Immigration Studies, Oct. 30, 2011. http://www.cis.org/feere/response-to-margaretstock.

[44] "Officers and Employees of Foreign Embassies and Consulates and their Families," U.S. Department of State Foreign Affairs Manual, 7 FAM 1116.2-2, November 30, 1995. www.docstoc.com/docs/8389457/Us-Citizen-ByBirth

[45] Jon Feere, "Birthright Citizenship in the United States: A Global Comparison," Center for Immigration Studies, Aug. 2010. http://www.cis.org/birthright-citizenship.

[46] "'Blue List' Cases — Children of Foreign Diplomats," U.S. Department of State Foreign Affairs Manual, 7 FAM 1111(d)(3), August 21, 2009. www.state.gov/documents/organization/86755.pdf.

In: Birthright Citizenship … ISBN: 978-1-63485-258-6
Editor: Garrett Manning

Chapter 6

TESTIMONY OF RICHARD COHEN, PRESIDENT, SOUTHERN POVERTY LAW CENTER. HEARING ON "BIRTHRIGHT CITIZENSHIP: IS IT THE RIGHT POLICY FOR AMERICA?"*

My name is Richard Cohen. I am an attorney and the president of the Southern Poverty Law Center. I have appeared in many state and federal courts, including the Supreme Court of the United States, and have testified on two prior occasions before congressional judiciary committees. I am honored to have been asked to testify today on the issue of birthright citizenship, and I hope that my testimony will be helpful to the subcommittee.

Founded in 1971 in Montgomery, Alabama, the birthplace of the modern civil rights movement, the Southern Poverty Law Center was founded to make the promise of the Fourteenth Amendment and the civil rights acts passed in the 1960s a reality in the Deep South. Since that time, we have represented tens of thousands of persons in cases ranging from racial desegregation to gender discrimination, from prison reform to children's rights, and from economic justice to LGBT equality.

In 2004, we established a project to address the needs of recent immigrants to our country. Since then, we have litigated numerous cases on behalf of exploited guest workers,[1] cases challenging harsh state laws designed

---

* This is an edited, reformatted and augmented version of testimony presented April 29, 2015 before the House Judiciary Committee, Subcommittee on Immigration and Border Security.

to push undocumented persons to deport themselves,[2] and cases involving the parental rights of immigrants. We also have had the privilege of representing children who owe their citizenship to the Citizenship Clause of the Fourteenth Amendment.

Wendy Ruiz was one such child. She was born and raised in Florida and graduated from a Florida high school. When she pursued her own American dream, Florida's public universities demanded that she pay higher tuition rates because her parents were undocumented.

Fortunately, Wendy was protected by one of the bedrock principles of our Constitution – the principle of citizenship by birth that is as old as this nation.[3] In 2012, the U.S. District Court for the Southern District of Florida recognized the rights of Wendy and other children of undocumented parents, holding that demanding higher tuition was against "a fundamental principle of American jurisprudence," that children should not be punished for the actions of their parents. *Ruiz v. Robinson*, 892 F.Supp.2d 1321, 1330 (S.D. Fl. 2012). The court went on to explain that "[o]bviously no child is responsible for his birth and penalizing the . . . child is an ineffectual – as well as unjust – way of deterring the parent." (citing *Plyler v. Doe*, 457 U.S. 202, 220 (1982)).

The "fundamental principle of American jurisprudence" to which the court in *Ruiz* referred finds expression in the Bible, *see e.g.*, Ezekiel 18:20, and, perhaps more importantly, for purposes of today's hearing, in the Fourteenth Amendment.

Passed in the aftermath of a war that claimed more than 600,000 lives, the Fourteenth Amendment provides that "All persons born or naturalized in the United States, and subject to the jurisdiction thereof, are citizens of the United States and of the State wherein they reside." The Amendment was intended, of course, to overrule the infamous *Dred Scott* decision and to ensure that former slaves born in this country would not be relegated to second-class citizenship. But the congressional debate surrounding the Citizenship Clause makes it absolutely clear that its reach was never intended to be limited solely to those persons previously held in servitude.

On May 29, 1866, amid debate in the Senate, Senator Jacob Howard of Michigan introduced an amendment clarifying that birthright citizenship would apply to everyone born within the United States with the exception of the children of foreign diplomats. Howard said that his amendment was "simply declaratory of what I regard as the law of the land already." This point was made clear during Senate debate over whether birthright citizenship would apply to children of all races and ethnicities. Cong. Globe, 39th Cong. 1st Session, 2890-92.

Just thirty years later, the Supreme Court interpreted the Citizenship Clause in a case involving the son of Chinese immigrants. Wong Kim Ark was born in San Francisco and had spent his entire life in the United States. When he was about 17, he traveled to China for a visit before returning home to San Francisco. When he returned to the United States after a second visit four years later, he was denied entry on the basis that he was allegedly not a citizen. Even though Congress had prohibited individuals of Chinese descent from becoming citizens, the Supreme Court held that the Fourteenth Amendment granted citizenship to all who were born in this country:

> The fourteenth amendment affirms the ancient and fundamental rule of citizenship by birth within the territory, in the allegiance and under the protection of the country . . . . The amendment, in clear words and in manifest intent, includes the children born within the territory of the United States of all other persons, of whatever race or color, domiciled within the United States. The fourteenth amendment . . . has conferred no authority upon congress to restrict the effect of birth, declared by the constitution to constitute a sufficient and complete right to citizenship.
>
> *United States v. Wong Kim Ark*, 169 U.S. 649, 703 (1898).

Nearly a century later, the Supreme Court relied on *Wong Kim Ark*'s interpretation of the Citizenship Clause in holding that, under the Equal Protection Clause, undocumented children are entitled to a public education. *Plyler v. Doe*, 457 U.S. 202 (1982). Although the majority in *Plyler* was a narrow one, the Court was unanimous in its conclusion that undocumented children in Texas were "within its jurisdiction" for purposes of the Equal Protection Clause of the Fourteenth Amendment. *Compare* 457 U.S. at 210-15 (opinion of the Court) *with* id. at 243 (dissent). In its analysis, the Court found that the meaning of the phrase "person within its jurisdiction" in the Equal Protection Clause is the same as "subject to the jurisdiction thereof" in the Citizenship Clause. Both, the Court said, are meant in a geographic sense, applying to anyone within the physical boundaries of the country. The Court quoted *Wong Kim Ark*'s finding that it was "impossible to construe the words 'subject to the jurisdiction thereof,' in the opening sentence [of the Fourteenth Amendment], as less comprehensive than the words 'within its jurisdiction,' in the concluding sentence of the same section; or to hold that persons 'within the jurisdiction' of one of the States of the Union are not 'subject to the jurisdiction' of the United States." *Plyler v. Doe*, 457 U.S. at 211 n. 10 (quoting *Wong Kim Ark*, 169 U.S. at 687).

Various legal scholars have made interesting arguments offering a different interpretation of the birthright citizenship clause.[4] But, to their credit, they have acknowledged that their arguments would require us to reject the understanding of the Citizenship Clause that has prevailed for more than 100 years.[5] Given that the Fourteenth Amendment was intended to put the issue of birthright citizenship beyond the reach of congressional legislation,[6] it would be quite anomalous at this late date to attempt to diminish or change the meaning of birthright citizenship other than by a constitutional amendment.

Amending the Constitution is a serious matter, one that requires great caution. Since the adoption of the Bill of Rights in conjunction with the Constitution's original ratification, our Constitution has been amended only 23 times in over 200 years. Before we take the momentous step of amending it again in order to limit birthright citizenship, we should carefully consider the reasons why the citizenship clause was originally enshrined in our Constitution.

From the beginning, our society has grappled with efforts to exclude certain categories of people from American citizenry. During the 1866 debate, Senator Edgar Cowan of Pennsylvania raged against the idea of children of Chinese immigrants and Gypsies becoming citizens by virtue of being born here, warning of a "flood of immigration of the Mongol race," an "inva[sion] by a flood of Australians or people from Borneo, man-eaters or cannibals," and Gypsies who "live nowhere, settle as trespassers wherever they go, and whose sole merit is a universal swindle." Senator Cowan urged his colleagues to restrict citizenship to people who resembled him, saying that "[i]f I desire the exercise of my rights I ought to go to my own people, the people of my own blood and lineage, people of the same religion, people of the same beliefs and traditions, and not thrust myself in upon a society of other men entirely different in all respects from myself." Cong. Globe, 39th Cong. 1st Session, 2890-91.

Senator John Conness of California rose in defense of the Amendment. He conceded that "it may be very good capital in an electioneering campaign to declaim against the Chinese." But he described Chinese immigrants as an "industrious people ... now passing from mining into other branches of industry and labor" including in "kitchens of hotels ... as farm hands in the fields ... [and] in building the Pacific railroad." Their children and those of Gypsies born in this country should be "regarded as citizens of the United States," he said. No person "claiming to have a high humanity," he argued, could take a contrary position. Cong. Globe, 39th Cong. 1st Session, 2892.

When the Supreme Court addressed birthright citizenship in *Wong Kim Ark*, the decision came during a period of tremendous backlash to Chinese immigration. Just 16 years earlier, President Arthur had signed the Chinese Exclusion Act, stopping the flow of Chinese laborers into the United States. It was the first such law to prevent a specific ethnic group from entering the country. Two major California papers expressed concern over the Supreme Court's decision. The *San Francisco Chronicle* warned that it "may have a wider effect upon the question of citizenship than the public supposes" because, the paper warned, "it is to be feared" that the birthright citizenship guarantee "may apply to Indians as well as Chinese."[7] A Los Angeles paper doubted the longevity of the decision, warning that it would only have an effect "if it remains the authoritative interpretation of the fourteenth amendment" and predicted that "[i]t is apparent that this decision will not be freely accepted as the last word on the subject."[8]

As *Wong Kim Ark* reflects, there has been tension in our country's history between the egalitarian principle underlying the Constitution's birthright citizenship clause and our nation's immigration policy. The former is animated by egalitarian ideas; the latter, all too often, has been animated by distinctions based on race and ethnicity. See Pres. Lyndon B. Johnson, Remarks at Signing of Immigration Bill, Liberty Island, N.Y. (Oct. 3, 1965) ("immigration policy of the United States has been distorted by the harsh injustice of the national origins quota system"). Today, we are witnessing another backlash to our nation's changing demographics and are engaged in serious debates about our immigration policy. Regardless of one's position on immigration policy questions, the sanctity of the birthright citizenship clause should not be disturbed. Any other course would risk creating a new class of second-class citizens.

This past fall, Wendy Ruiz, our client in the Florida tuition case I mentioned earlier in my testimony, spoke at the Dexter Avenue King Memorial Baptist Church, the church from which Dr. King and his allies launched the modern civil rights movement, the Second American Revolution. She told a deeply American story, one about her family's struggles and her commitment to get an education to help others in her community. It is simply inconceivable to me that our country would deny the blessings of citizenship to the Wendy Ruizes of the world.

Thank you.

End Notes

[1] See, e.g., Andy Grimm, Indian Workers in Labor Trafficking Lawsuit Win $14 Million in New Orleans Federal Court, NOLA.com, Times-Picayune (Feb. 18, 2015, 4:32 PM), http://www.nola.com/crime/ index.ssf/2015/02/federal_jury_in_new_orleans_aw.html.

[2] See, e.g., Hispanic Interest Coalition of Alabama v. Governor of Alabama, 691 F.3d 1236 (11th Cir. 2012) (finding that a provision of Alabama's H.B. 56 substantially burdened a constitutional right of undocumented children).

[3] In 1830, the Supreme Court wrote that if a person "was born [in the independent United States], he was born an American citizen, whether his parents were at the time of his birth British subjects or American citizens. Nothing is better settled at the common law than the doctrine that the children even of aliens born in a country, while the parents are resident there under the protection of the government, and owing a temporary allegiance thereto, are subjects by birth." Inglis v. Trustees of Sailor's Snug Harbor, 28 U.S. 99 (1830).

[4] See, e.g., Peter H. Schuck & Rogers M. Smith, Citizenship Without Consent: Illegal Aliens in the American Polity, (New Haven: Yale University Press 1985); Lino A. Graglia, Birthright Citizenship for Children of Illegal Aliens: An Irrational Public Policy, 14 Tex. Rev. L. & Pol. 1 (2009); John C. Eastman, From Feudalism to Consent: Rethinking Birthright Citizenship, Legal Memorandum (The Heritage Foundation), Mar. 30, 2006, available at http://www.heritage.org/research/reports/2006/03/from-feudalism-to-consent-rethinking-birthright-citizenship.

[5] See Peter H. Schuck, Birthright of a Nation, N.Y. Times, Aug. 14, 2010, at A19 ([T]he Fourteenth Amendment has "traditionally been interpreted to give automatic citizenship to anyone born on American soil, even to the children of illegal immigrants."); Graglia, Birthright Citizenship, at 2 ("American law, as currently understood, provides an enormous inducement to illegal immigration: namely an automatic grant of American citizenship to the children of illegal immigrants born in this country."); Eastman, From Feudalism ("It is today routinely believed that under the Citizenship Clause of the Fourteenth Amendment, mere birth on U.S. soil is sufficient to obtain U.S. citizenship.").

[6] See Wong Kim Ark, 169 U.S. at 703 ("The power of naturalization, vested in congress by the constitution, is a power to confer citizenship, not a power to take it away. . . . The fourteenth amendment, while it leaves the power, where it was before, in congress, to regulate naturalization, has conferred no authority upon congress to restrict the effect of birth, declared by the constitution to constitute a sufficient and complete right to citizenship.").

[7] Questions of Citizenship, S.F. Chron., March 30, 1898, available at http://upload.wikimedia.org/wikipedia/commons/0/08/Wong_Kim_Ark_editorial_San_Francisco_Chronicle_1898- 03-30.png.

[8] Enoch Knight, Citizen Wong Kim Ark, The Herald, July 24, 1898, 17, available at http://chroniclingamerica.loc.gov/lccn/sn85042461/1898-07-24/ed-1/seq17/#date1=1897&index=0&rows=20&words=ARK+KIM+WONG&searchType=basic&sequence=0&state=California&date2=1899&proxtext=%22Wong+Kim+Ark%22&y=8&x=19&dateFilterType=yearRange&page=1.

INDEX

#

21st century, 2

A

ABA, 52
abuse, 60
access, 85, 89
accommodations, 88
advocacy, 102
affirming, 27
Afghanistan, 13, 27, 33, 35, 67
African Americans, 34, 39, 41
African-American, 69
age, 23, 27, 84, 87, 88, 95, 96, 102, 103
agencies, 91, 94, 98, 99, 100, 101
ambassadors, 7, 9, 71, 74, 76, 77, 81
American Bar Association, 36
American Bar Association (ABA), 36
American Samoa, 14, 20, 28, 45
ancestors, 39
annotation, 59
antitrust, 81
armed forces, 20, 80
Asia, 103
assimilation, 40, 95
asylum, 31
Attorney General, 50, 59, 69, 81
authorities, 10, 49, 56, 58
authority, 2, 11, 12, 14, 21, 22, 42, 65, 72, 78, 79, 99, 109, 112

B

backlash, 111
ban, 19, 31
Barbados, 87
benefits, 13, 56, 84, 85, 93, 94
Bible, 108
births, 56, 83, 96, 98
blogs, 103
blood, 3, 36, 110
Brazil, 89
brothers, 84

C

candidates, 34, 35
case law, 2, 15, 18, 20, 22, 28, 54, 60
cash, 103
CDC, 96, 98
Census, 24, 55, 97
certificate, 36, 52, 96, 97, 99, 100
challenges, 44
chemical, 68
Chicago, 80
Chief Justice, 6, 11, 28, 73
children, vii, 1, 2, 3, 4, 5, 6, 7, 8, 9, 10, 11, 12, 13, 15, 17, 18, 19, 20, 21, 24, 25, 26,

27, 28, 30, 31, 33, 34, 35, 37, 40, 41, 42, 43, 48, 49, 50, 51, 52, 54, 56, 59, 60, 64, 65, 68, 71, 73, 74, 76, 77, 78, 79, 80, 81, 83, 84, 85, 86, 87, 88, 89, 90, 98, 99, 100, 101, 102, 107, 108, 109, 110, 112
China, 9, 11, 30, 42, 75, 85, 94, 103, 104, 109
Chinese government, 95
CIS, 56
citizens, vii, 1, 3, 4, 5, 6, 7, 8, 9, 12, 13, 19, 20, 22, 23, 25, 26, 27, 29, 30, 31, 32, 34, 35, 37, 38, 39, 40, 43, 44, 45, 46, 47, 49, 50, 53, 56, 57, 60, 63, 64, 68, 69, 70, 71, 72, 73, 74, 75, 77, 78, 80, 81, 83, 84, 85, 86, 88, 90, 91, 94, 95, 97, 98, 99, 101, 108, 109, 110, 112
citizenship, vii, 1, 2, 3, 4, 5, 6, 7, 8, 9, 10, 11, 12, 13, 14, 15, 16, 17, 18, 19, 20, 21, 22, 23, 24, 25, 26, 27, 28, 30, 31, 32, 33, 34, 35, 36, 37, 38, 39, 40, 41, 42, 43, 44, 45, 46, 47, 48, 49, 50, 51, 52, 53, 55, 56, 57, 58, 60, 61, 63, 64, 65, 67, 68, 69, 70, 73, 74, 75, 76, 77, 78, 79, 80, 81, 83, 84, 85, 86, 87, 88, 89, 90, 91, 92, 95, 96, 98, 99, 100, 101, 102, 103, 104, 105, 107, 108, 109, 110, 111, 112
civil rights, 41, 107, 111
Civil War, 2, 5, 6, 10, 38, 53
clarity, 45, 83, 89, 102
classes, 60, 77
classification, 81
clothing, 24
CNN, 97, 104
color, iv, 10, 23, 40, 45, 109
common law, 2, 3, 5, 6, 10, 11, 14, 16, 25, 30, 36, 37, 38, 42, 50, 57, 60, 64, 112
Commonwealth of the Northern Mariana Islands, 24
communities, 9, 74
community, 2, 39, 40, 42, 43, 111
conflict, 79
congress, 59, 109, 112
Congress, iv, 5, 6, 11, 14, 19, 20, 21, 22, 23, 24, 27, 28, 30, 31, 32, 33, 34, 35, 36, 37, 38, 42, 44, 45, 48, 49, 51, 53, 57, 60, 61, 65, 68, 69, 70, 72, 78, 79, 80, 83, 84, 85, 86, 89, 90, 91, 92, 96, 98, 99, 103, 109
consent, 2, 14, 16, 17, 18, 30, 38, 54, 64, 77, 78, 85, 112
conspiracy, 93, 104
Constitution, vii, 1, 3, 5, 6, 7, 8, 10, 11, 12, 14, 15, 19, 20, 21, 24, 25, 26, 28, 29, 31, 33, 34, 35, 37, 38, 39, 42, 43, 44, 45, 49, 52, 53, 54, 60, 61, 63, 64, 65, 68, 69, 73, 78, 79, 81, 88, 90, 91, 108, 110, 111
constitutional amendment, 2, 4, 5, 14, 19, 21, 23, 31, 32, 34, 44, 46, 48, 51, 60, 71, 89, 90, 110
constitutional issues, 20, 47
constitutional law, 21
constitutional principles, 4
construction, 32
contradiction, 77
controversies, 42
counsel, 48, 79
Court of Appeals, 12, 14, 21, 90
covering, 53
criticism, 57
Cuba, 67

D

damages, iv
data set, 99
database, 99
Democrat, 86, 90
denial, 31, 64
Department of Homeland Security, 84
Department of Justice, 31, 81
destruction, 23
detention, 27, 67, 81
discrimination, 107
divergence, 22
Dominican Republic, 86, 89
dream, 108
drug trafficking, 93
due process, 47, 48, 88

E

economic downturn, 84
education, 12, 94, 111
election, 22, 53
e-mail, 100
embassy, 100
employees, 101
employers, 87
employment, 88, 100
enemies, 10, 11, 60, 78, 82
enemy combatants, 27, 34, 35, 68
enforcement, 9, 49, 56, 81, 84, 87, 91, 92, 93, 95, 97
England, 5, 37, 42, 53, 60
enrollment, 12
equality, 31, 107
ethnicity, 33, 35, 39, 41, 111
Europe, 61
evidence, 16, 42, 47, 71, 72, 81, 89, 92, 93, 97
exclusion, 6, 17, 26, 30, 40, 61
executive branch, 10, 92
exercise, 72, 78, 110
exporters, 81
expulsion, 26

F

fairness, 54
families, 7, 71, 81
family members, 33, 61, 89, 94
fear, 41, 84
federal courts, 2, 4, 49, 60, 107
federal government, 92, 93
Federal Government, 65
federal law, 38
fertility, 50
fidelity, 77
Fifth Amendment, 28, 81
Fiji, 89
financial, 23, 93
food, 85
force, 14, 25, 34, 37, 102
Ford, 32
foreign nationals, 74, 77, 78
formation, 39
Fourteenth Amendment, vii, 1, 2, 3, 4, 7, 8, 9, 10, 11, 12, 13, 14, 15, 16, 17, 18, 21, 22, 23, 26, 28, 29, 30, 31, 32, 33, 34, 35, 36, 37, 39, 40, 41, 42, 43, 44, 46, 48, 49, 50, 51, 52, 54, 56, 57, 60, 61, 63, 64, 68, 69, 70, 71, 72, 73, 74, 75, 76, 77, 78, 80, 107, 108, 109, 110, 112
framing, 17
fraud, 92, 93, 94, 95, 96, 103, 104
funds, 12

G

grand jury, 28
grants, 22, 86, 88, 92
Great Britain, 25, 65
growth, 84, 87, 92
Guam, 24, 56
Guantanamo, 67
guesthouses, 88
guidance, 102
guidelines, 81, 101, 102
guilty, 82

H

hair, 94
Hawaii, 95
health, 94
health care, 94
high school, 95, 108
history, vii, 2, 4, 5, 10, 13, 15, 17, 20, 23, 25, 35, 42, 54, 60, 69, 71, 77, 79, 81, 91, 111
homes, 97
honesty, 95
hospitality, 60
host, 94
hotel, 94
hotels, 88, 110

House, 7, 8, 10, 19, 20, 23, 24, 28, 30, 31, 32, 42, 51, 52, 53, 54, 60, 63, 64, 67, 73, 75, 76, 80, 81, 83, 107
House of Representatives, 54, 60
human, 68, 88
human right, 88
human rights, 88
husband, 54

I

ideals, 17
identification, 99
illegal aliens, 18, 30, 61, 64, 65, 84, 85, 86, 87, 88, 89, 90, 93, 99
images, 104
immigrants, 23, 29, 41, 50, 60, 65, 79, 83, 84, 85, 87, 88, 89, 93, 101, 102, 107, 109, 110, 112
immigration, vii, 1, 3, 7, 9, 18, 19, 30, 31, 33, 35, 36, 40, 45, 49, 51, 56, 59, 64, 68, 79, 84, 85, 86, 87, 88, 89, 90, 91, 92, 93, 94, 95, 101, 102, 103, 110, 111, 112
Immigration and Nationality Act, 4, 19, 21, 23, 24, 33, 35, 43, 59, 61, 65, 90
immunity, 3, 37
imprisonment, 93
income, 93
independence, 28, 37, 53
Independence, 5, 37, 42
India, 86
Indians, 6, 9, 26, 30, 39, 40, 41, 42, 43, 70, 72, 74, 76, 82, 111
individuals, 71, 90, 93, 95, 109
industry, 85, 92, 110
inferences, 17
inheritance, 5, 54
injury, iv
INS, 28, 32
insertion, 41
interest groups, 19
international law, 58, 76, 102
International Monetary Fund, 86
investment, 94, 103, 104
Ireland, 38, 86
issues, 3, 12, 14, 15, 19, 21, 22, 46, 47, 50, 64, 101

J

Jackson Lee, Sheila, 103
Johnson, Andrew, 7
Johnson, Lyndon Baines, 111
Jordan, 52, 104
judicial branch, 21
Judicial Branch, 31
judicial interpretation, 49, 79
judicial power, 79
judiciary, 107
Judiciary Committee, 20, 63, 67, 83, 107
jurisdiction, vii, 1, 2, 3, 4, 7, 8, 9, 11, 12, 13, 14, 16, 17, 18, 19, 22, 23, 27, 30, 32, 33, 34, 35, 37, 39, 41, 42, 43, 46, 47, 48, 49, 51, 56, 60, 63, 64, 68, 69, 70, 71, 72, 73, 74, 75, 76, 77, 78, 79, 80, 81, 82, 86, 88, 90, 93, 98, 99, 102, 108, 109
justification, 22

L

laws, 2, 12, 16, 27, 34, 37, 38, 39, 41, 42, 45, 49, 51, 53, 57, 58, 69, 72, 76, 77, 88, 89, 93, 102, 103
lead, 6, 10, 69, 71
legality, 27, 84
legislation, vii, 11, 30, 31, 32, 35, 36, 44, 45, 48, 49, 52, 54, 57, 58, 82, 85, 86, 90, 103, 110
legislative proposals, 15, 56
light, 5, 10, 22, 23, 82, 90
litigation, 91
longevity, 111
Louisiana, 13, 32, 33, 35, 67, 69, 72, 81
low-interest loans, 94

M

magnet, 68
magnets, 79

mainstream society, 43
majority, 5, 8, 16, 27, 32, 50, 53, 54, 56, 61, 73, 109
marriage, 54, 58
Maryland, 40, 55
mass, 84
matter, iv, 32, 44, 65, 68, 69, 75, 90, 91, 100, 110
media, 34, 35, 85, 103
Medicaid, 85
membership, 16
meter, 29
Mexico, 86, 88
middle class, 85
migration, 33, 35, 84, 89, 95
military, 67, 70
minors, 50
miscarriage, 98
Missouri, 40
Montana, 52
Moon, 59

N

national origin, 34, 111
national security, 33, 35
nationality, 3, 35, 58, 80, 88
Native Americans, 3, 6, 20, 24, 25, 26, 34, 41, 43, 51, 56
neutral, 27
New Zealand, 86
Nigeria, 85

O

Obama Administration, 23, 91
Obama, President Barack, 90
obedience, 77
obstacles, 21, 22
officials, 67, 88, 92, 94, 99, 100, 101
Oklahoma, 52, 56
operations, 81, 103
original visa, 91

P

Pacific, 110
Paraguay, 88
parallel, 45, 46, 61
parentage, 7, 26, 47
parents, vii, 1, 2, 3, 5, 6, 7, 9, 11, 13, 18, 19, 20, 23, 24, 25, 27, 29, 30, 32, 33, 34, 35, 36, 38, 39, 40, 41, 42, 44, 45, 48, 49, 50, 51, 52, 56, 57, 67, 68, 70, 73, 75, 76, 77, 78, 79, 80, 84, 85, 87, 88, 89, 91, 95, 96, 98, 99, 102, 108, 112
permission, iv, 88
permit, 12, 21, 23, 47, 60, 79, 81, 87
Peru, 88
Philippines, 28
PM, 112
police, 50, 102
policy, 3, 10, 15, 16, 18, 20, 21, 68, 79, 87, 88, 90, 92, 95, 96, 101, 111
political power, 72
politics, 32, 52
pollution, 94
population, 41, 84, 88, 89, 97
precedent, 4, 8, 20, 21, 22, 37, 75
precedents, 22
preparation, iv
president, 84, 88, 91, 107
President, vi, 5, 7, 25, 27, 37, 52, 90, 107, 111
prima facie, 50
principles, 6, 10, 13, 25, 30, 31, 38, 57, 108
project, 68, 107
property rights, 88
proposition, 7
protection, 4, 10, 11, 12, 13, 16, 25, 37, 41, 47, 48, 50, 58, 109, 112
public concern, 35
public education, 109
public policy, 60
Puerto Rico, 24, 28, 56
punishment, 104

Q

qualifications, 10, 23
quotas, 50

R

race, 6, 8, 10, 23, 33, 35, 39, 40, 41, 109, 110, 111
ratification, 34, 37, 45, 46, 72, 73, 81, 110
reading, 11, 70, 79, 81
reality, 107
reasoning, 102
recall, 67
reciprocity, 54
recognition, 79
recommendations, iv, 87
redistricting, 3
redundancy, 69
reform, 35, 56, 107
Reform, 60, 103
refugees, 20
Registry, 81
regulations, 99
rejection, 76
relatives, 56
relevance, 71
relief, 23
religion, 110
requirement, 11, 32, 41, 50, 63, 77, 80, 98
requirements, 6, 17, 47, 53, 58, 68
researchers, 99
resolution, 36, 52, 79
response, 6, 57, 71, 72, 82, 84, 85, 100, 105
restrictions, 20, 23, 34, 35, 42, 64
retirement, 92, 94
rights, iv, 8, 13, 21, 24, 34, 35, 48, 54, 61, 64, 90, 107, 108, 110
rings, 104
risk, 68, 87, 111
rule of law, 22
rules, 10, 88, 102

S

sabotage, 78
Samoa, 14, 28
Saudi Arabia, 61, 68
scholarship, 4
school, 12, 95
scope, 2, 4, 8, 14, 15, 17, 18, 22, 34, 41, 48, 49, 52, 75, 84, 86, 89, 90, 93, 98, 99, 104
second-class citizens, 108, 111
Senate, 7, 19, 41, 52, 53, 71, 108
services, iv, 94, 97
shores, 77
siblings, 35, 96
slaves, 6, 19, 39, 61, 78, 108
social contract, 17
social fabric, 95
Social Security, 83, 91, 97, 98, 99
Social Security Administration, 99
social welfare, 96
society, 37, 110
South America, 3
sovereign state, 54
sovereignty, 10, 13, 27, 67, 76, 80
specter, 40
SSA, 99
stars, 85
state, 8, 10, 12, 14, 19, 22, 25, 26, 36, 37, 38, 39, 43, 44, 48, 52, 53, 58, 61, 73, 77, 98, 102, 105, 107, 112
state laws, 37, 38, 39, 44, 48, 53, 107
states, 3, 4, 6, 8, 24, 25, 31, 34, 36, 37, 38, 45, 51, 52, 53, 54, 60, 63, 69, 74, 80, 88, 104
statistics, 56
statutes, 5, 18, 26, 32, 34, 37, 38, 43, 92
statutory provisions, 44
suicide, 63
Supreme Court, 2, 4, 5, 6, 8, 9, 12, 13, 14, 15, 16, 17, 18, 22, 24, 34, 36, 39, 42, 43, 46, 48, 50, 51, 52, 55, 58, 64, 65, 67, 68, 69, 73, 74, 75, 79, 80, 81, 83, 91, 107, 109, 111, 112

T

Taiwan, 95
takeover, 40
Taliban, 33, 35, 58, 67
target, 4, 8, 103
tax evasion, 93
taxation, 40, 41
taxes, 96
taxpayers, 94
techniques, 94
temporary protection, 37
tension, 111
territorial, 2, 9, 10, 16, 24, 30, 36, 71, 72, 74, 75, 76, 77, 79
territory, 2, 3, 5, 10, 14, 23, 28, 37, 38, 54, 69, 74, 76, 78, 89, 109
terrorism, 68, 81, 93
textbook, 30
thoughts, 90
Title V, 58
tourism, 3, 34, 35, 36, 51, 84, 85, 86, 90, 92, 93, 94, 95, 96, 97, 103, 104
tracks, 4, 78
trade, 68
traditions, 110
trafficking, 68
transmission, 58
treaties, 8, 26, 34, 42, 43
trial, 28
tuition, 94, 96, 108, 111
Turkey, 85

U

U.S. immigration law, 49
uniform, 5
United Kingdom, 57, 86
United Nations, 102
United States, i, iii, v, vii, 1, 2, 3, 4, 5, 6, 7, 8, 9, 10, 11, 12, 13, 14, 15, 16, 17, 18, 19, 20, 22, 23, 24, 25, 26, 27, 28, 29, 30, 31, 32, 33, 34, 35, 36, 37, 38, 39, 40, 41, 42, 43, 44, 45, 46, 47, 48, 49, 50, 51, 52, 53, 55, 56, 58, 59, 60, 61, 63, 64, 65, 68,레69, 70, 71, 73, 74, 75, 76, 77, 78, 79, 80, 81, 82, 83, 84, 85, 86, 89, 90, 91, 93, 94, 95, 96, 97, 98, 99, 100, 102, 103, 104, 105, 107, 108, 109, 110, 111, 112
universities, 108
USA, 97, 104

V

variations, 44, 87
Verdugo-Urquidez, 28
vessels, 24
veto, 7
Vice President, 37
Victims of Trafficking, 20
violent crime, 91
visa system, 91
visa systems, 91
voting, 22

W

wages, 87
walking, 94
war, 33, 35, 78, 82, 108
welfare, 85, 103
wholesale, 50
Wisconsin, 55, 71
witnesses, 20, 54
workers, 107
World War I, 12

Y

Yale University, 28, 112